D1028433

CHINA
TOWARDS
THE YEAR
2000

NEW WORLD PRESS   BEIJING, CHINA

First Edition 1989

ISBN 7-80005-092-0/Z · 022

Published by
NEW WORLD PRESS
24 Baiwanzhuang Road, Beijing, China

Printed by
FOREIGN LANGUAGES PRINTING HOUSE
19 Chegongzhuang Xilu, Beijing, China

Distributed by
CHINA INTERNATIONAL BOOK TRADING CORPORATION
21 Chegongzhuang Xilu, Beijing, China
P.O. Box 399, Beijing, China Postal Zone: 100044

Printed in the People's Republic of China

CONTENTS

INTRODUCTION

This book is a very brief yet comprehensive summary of the research work we have done, such as "China Towards the Year 2000," "Industrial Policy and Industrial Restructuring" and other research papers. We tried to integrate these materials in a systematic and readable form. We shall describe here the background of our two major research projects, the source of this book and the interrelations between them. This will help readers to understand more clearly the meaning and intention of our presentation.

Academically, the "China Towards the Year 2000" study belongs to the discipline of futurology. Since the founding of the World Future Society in 1966, future studies has emerged as a new discipline which is defined as "a component of policy science concentrating on normative research into alternative future outcomes and policies." This science is maturing as evidenced by the World Future Society's Sixth General Assembly and Exposition. All its sessions dealt with practical problems facing the people of the world in the 1990s and beyond. A "Futures in Education" conference held in Melbourne in 1986 and a session of "A Future Studies Program Update" held at the Sixth General Assembly discussed the problems of initiation, administration and development of a program of future science and technology. How to transfer this new discipline to the modernization process of China is one of the targets of the opening of China, and it is also the responsibility of policy research organizations.

The former Technical Economic Research Center of the State Council, which we two were associated with, initiated the project "China Towards the Year 2000" under a directive from China's leadership, not purely for academic interest but also because this project had practical importance for national development.

1

China has achieved economic development through the means of economic planning. It is necessary to point out here that people in general believe, erroneously, that economic planning is done only in socialist countries. In the decade since World War II, the pursuit of economic development has been marked by the almost universal acceptance of certain types of development planning as the most direct route to economic progress. Not only has national planning become much more pervasive, but also the planning department is now an indispensable component in the organization charts of many Western corporations. This widespread practice is the result of a confluence of historical factors, the increasing complexity and uncertainty of a modern world and the conception of how best to adapt to a changing world. Some Western historians note that the Five-Year Plans and the Great Depression stand out in the inter-war period, the one accentuating the other, and each having repercussions that are being felt to the present day. At the end of World War II, the U.S.S.R. emerged as the No. 2 world power, using central planning and national control to transform its economy from a predominantly agrarian state to near-modernity in just 30 years. The Indian leaders, with intellectual roots in British socialism, also encouraged national planning. Her planning period is exactly the same as that of China; she is now also in the Seventh Five-Year Planning period. The success of the Marshall Plan in reconstructing Europe was attributed to the ample provision of capital and cooperative planning by the European countries. The widespread influence of Keynesian economics, which encouraged macro-economic forecasting and fiscal planning, also helped stimulate development planning.

In short, as an objective law adopted by nations or enterprises, planning is a useful tool for adapting to a changing environment, for if we could first know where we are, and whether we are tending, we could better judge what to do, and how to do it.

There are many types of planning and techniques available now—strategic planning, long-range planning, medium-term and annual planning, comprehensive planning, sectorial planning, etc. Regarding planning techniques, there are now available many mathematical tools for forecasting, optimizing and evaluating alternative development goals; many group exploration techniques have also been developed for making qualitative judgments. And there is now abundant international literature which discusses innovative methods and experiences in integrated development, taking into consideration social and even cultural factors.

Although China has implemented medium-term economic planning for more than three decades, there is much room for further improvement of our planning practices. This is one of the essential aspects in our national development.

We have conducted our project "China Towards the Year 2000" with the above points in mind. This study represents an effort by us to carry out a long-term development study which would complement the work done by the routine planning agency. Our studies examine many major national and global sectors in a comprehensive way—projecting future trends in some essential and carefully chosen areas such as population and employment, the economy in general, consumption and consumption patterns, energy, natural resources, agriculture, transport, ecological environment, international environment (economic and political), education, science and technology, foreign trade and health. The interaction among them is analyzed in the main report and quantitative analysis report. (These areas are abbreviated in Chapters II, III and VII). Also, this study is long-term in outlook as opposed to our routine "five-year" plans. Our study tries to evaluate the alternative futures in terms of economic, ecological and social sustainability, and policy recommendations are given for overall national development and in different sectors (Chapters IX and X).

The "China Towards the Year 2000" study, although experimental in nature, is a successful and leading one internationally. We introduced this project at the opening session of the "Europerspective" meeting attended by 1,500 participants in Paris in 1986 and also at the World Future Society's Sixth General Assembly and Exposition in Washington D.C., July 1989. There are now around 40 countries and regions who have carried out such "21st Century Studies." There is a growing trend for other countries to enter into this type of study.

Though we appear to be leading in this field at present, we are not satisfied with our experimental work. We have not carried out study of the social aspects of our report in detail. And the "China Towards the Year 2000" study covers too wide a scope; deeper study in one sector will be helpful and provide practical significance for national development.

On this basis, we have continued to carry out the project "Industrial Policy and Industrial Restructuring" after our completion of the study "China Towards the Year 2000."

As part of our reform process, there have been arguments about the merits of the market versus planning due to insufficient understanding of historical facts. Some consider industrial policy a type of government intervention which contradicts the development of market. Industrial policy has long been appreciated by and adopted in the Federal Republic of Germany, France and Japan. There are debates about industrial policy among Western economists, but a report done by the University of Pennsylvania Economic Research Unit under the sponsorship of the U.S. Department of Commerce during 1980-1982 concluded, "Although new technologies may go a long way towards redressing the industrial world's problems, there is no assurance that market processes will automatically effect the required structural changes. It has become widely recognized, as a consequence, that explicit policies will be needed if a continuation and worsening of this situation is to be avoided in the 1980s. Such policies include those aimed at increasing the economic supply potential (that is, increasing resources, labor supply and capital stock), developing technology, fostering industrial development, improving mobility and structure adaptation, etc. Frequently these policies have been called industrial policies...." This statement illustrates the fact that the industrial policy is now also a central concern even for typical market-oriented economies such as that of the U.S.A. Thus, there is no conflict between industrial policy and the market.

It is our intention to continue the "Industrial Policy and

Industrial Restructuring" study as an in-depth study of selected sectors which are of importance to national development.

The study of "Industrial Policy and Industrial Restructuring" is also a joint research project between the Development Research Center and the World Bank. But the project is still continuing. We only present in Chapter V some of the background materials which we have done in the initial phase of this joint research project. We hope we can report to our readers in the future about the research results after the completion of that project. But the integrated treatment of these two subjects as presented in this book will show our basic philosophy on policy study.

We consider our research work as a continuous "learning by doing" process. We have tried to carry out our research in different stages and not in isolation. Also, doing research on a selected subject, we have studied the historical trends and current situations of that subject both domestically and internationally, realizing that international experience should not be applied blindly but should be properly combined with the concrete conditions of China. A continuous improvement of the research is necessary through information feedbacks, i.e., we must monitor the research results in application and modify those points which are not fitted to real conditions.

With this basic philosophy in mind, we sincerely welcome any criticisms from our readers.

We should also like to thank our colleagues at the center and all the other institutions who have contributed to these two projects, because we have drawn freely upon the materials contained in them. We also wish to express our thanks to the editors of New World Press for their efforts in publishing this material.

Wang Huijiong
Li Boxi
August 1989

CHAPTER I
CHINA IS SHAPING ITS FUTURE

Section 1
Basic Estimation of the International Environment In the Years to Come

After decades of socialist construction, New China has emerged in the world arena as a force to be reckoned with, both politically and economically. With the introduction of the policy of opening to the outside world, business people the world over have flocked to China to seek new opportunities. How China's economy will fare in the future is thus of worldwide interest. The 12th National Congress of the Chinese Communist Party set forth the goal of quadrupling China's gross annual value of the industrial and agricultural output value (based on that of 1980) by the end of this century. Studying the development strategy and forecasting the future will help in achieving this strategic objective. In so doing, we have to understand the conditions of our country and the trends of world development. In other words, we have to formulate the development strategy of our country and its various regions in the midst of global changes.

According to "The International Environment for China Towards the Year 2000," a treatise adopted at the Beijing Conference on the Asian-Pacific Economy Towards the Year 2000, the following projections can be made in regard to the international environment for China around the turn of the century.

1. The present pattern of three worlds will continue, and no fundamental change is expected in this century

The Soviet Union and the United States will go on contending for world hegemony. By the year 2000, the two countries will remain the most powerful states in the world, militarily and economically. In the decade to come, no other country can take their place, but neither of the two powers will be strong enough to predominate over its adversary. However, with the emergence of Japan and Western Europe as two new economic giants and the economic growth of some developing countries, the grip of the Soviet Union and the United States on world affairs has been weakened, and this trend will continue in the years to come. The tripartite competition among the United States, Japan and Western Europe in the economic sphere will intensify. The Soviet Union, which has exercised rigid control over its East European allies by dint of its military might, is also likely to adopt new approaches in its relations with these countries, especially in the face of the progress made in its economic reforms.

The third world countries will have a greater say in world political affairs. Their fight against imperialism and hegemonism will continue to be the mainstream in the future development of world politics. However, their joint struggle will be beset by twists and turns as the superpowers will take advantage of the contradictions among the third world countries to sow discord to consolidate their own dominant position. While the possibility of intensified Soviet-US rivalry leading to a world war cannot be ruled out entirely, it is unlikely that a global conflict will break out in the remaining years of this century. This is because the two superpowers are evenly matched in strength, their control over their allies is weakening, and the struggles waged by the people all over the world for peace and against war is gathering momentum.

The political situation in the areas around our country is favorable to us. After the return of Hong Kong to the motherland, the Taiwan issue will become all the more outstanding. The reunification of Taiwan with the mainland of China is an inevitable trend. A large-scale, local war directly involving China is highly improbable.

All in all, despite the existence of some unstable factors, it is entirely possible for us to achieve a relatively stable, peaceful international environment for national construction so long as we adhere to our independent and flexible foreign policy and turn all the favorable conditions to our account.

2. Although the basic pattern of three worlds remains unchanged, the world economy will move further towards multi-polarization

As for the developed capitalist countries, the tripartite competition among the United States, Japan, and Western Europe will intensify, and the trend of multi-polarization of the capitalist world economy will become even more irreversible. As competition becomes fiercer, the protectionist trend in trade will gain ground. Owing to the economic malaise in the developed capitalist countries, especially the record high fiscal deficits, high interest rates, and huge trade imbalance of the United States, and the difficulties confronting the developing countries in servicing their debts, the possibility of an international financial crisis cannot be excluded. The developed countries will rely more heavily on the markets of the developing countries, and their struggles for markets in the third world countries will become more acute.

The Soviet Union is far stronger than other East European countries economically. Although its control over other member states of the Council for Mutual Economic Assistance (CMEA) is weakening, the East European countries cannot yet form an economic bloc to contend with the Soviet Union. There is increasing contact between East European countries and the developed capitalist countries. In spite of the restrictions and obstructions by the two superpowers, closer economic ties will develop between East and West European countries. At the same time, there will be increasing economic contact between East and West European countries on the one hand and the developing countries on the other.

As a whole, the developing countries will continue to develop economically even in the face of great difficulties. Economic cooperation among them will be further strengthened in the future. Meanwhile, the economic ties between developing countries and developed countries will also become closer. As we forge ahead in national construction, our economic relations and cooperation with other developing countries will be consolidated further.

It is generally acknowledged that the Asian-Pacific region is the most dynamic economic theater in the world. The countries in East and Southeast Asia as a whole have been able to maintain a very high rate of economic growth since 1960. The so-called "newly industrialized countries (areas)" in the region achieved the highest growth rate in the world throughout the 1960s and 1970s. Although Japan's economy has lost its momentum of the 1960s, its performance is still the best among the developed countries. The Asian-Pacific region has shown exceptional dynamism even during a worldwide recession. In 1979-82, when the capitalist world was plunged into the most severe economic crisis since the crash of the 1930s, most Asian-Pacific countries managed to maintain their economic growth, though at a slower pace. Owing to the excellent economic performance of these countries, the center of the world's economy has begun to shift towards this region. However, it is unlikely the region will replace the Atlantic region as the center of the world's economy within this century. Meanwhile, the economic conflicts between Japan and the Unites States in this region are sharpening, and the West European countries are also showing growing interest in this region. This state of affairs provides us with an opportunity to increase our economic contact with these countries as well as to take advantage of the contradictions among them to quicken the tempo of our economic development.

It is thus clear that the changes in the economic patterns of the world in the years to come are favorable to China's modernization drive.

3.   Different estimations and forecasts about the prospects of the growth of the world economy

An optimistic estimate holds that developments in science

and technology, the readjustment of the economic structure, and changes in economic policy will bring about another round of high-speed economic growth for the developed capitalist countries which will in tun propel the world economy to grow at a relatively high speed. Another estimate maintains that the growth of the world economy hereafter will continue at a low rate, probably similar to that of the 1970s. In our study of this problem, more people are inclined to favor the latter possibility. These people made the following rough estimate of the growth of the world economy: Between 1980 and 2000, the average annual growth rate of the world economy, in terms of gross national product (GNP), is likely to be the same or slightly faster than that of the 1970s, with that of the developed capitalist countries standing at about 3 percent, the Soviet Union and other East European countries about 4 percent, and the developing countries about 5 percent.

The economic situation in the Asian-Pacific region has and will continue to have an important bearing on the Chinese economy. The prospects for economic development in the region is one of the most important external conditions for China's economic growth in the years to come.

Section 2
Meet Challenge With Challenge

There are several major trends in the world today. They are having and will continue to have a tremendous impact on the development of China and the world as a whole. Given the push of these trends, what strategy is to be adopted and what countermeasures are to be taken have a vital bearing on the rise or fall of a country, a region, or even a city.

Of these trends, there are three most important ones: the worldwide technological revolution; the reform in the socialist countries; and the movement of the center of the world economy towards the Pacific.

1. The worldwide technological revolution

There are several different ways in describing this trend. Some people call it the fourth industrial revolution. The first refers to the invention and wide application of weaving machines and steam engines in the second half of the eighteenth century. There is a consensus of opinion on this point. Some people hold that the second industrial revolution took place in the second half of the nineteenth century and the beginning of this century. It was marked by the application of electricity, including the emergence of electrical machinery and telecommunications and the introduction of motor cars and railways. The third industrial revolution is said to have taken place after World War II and was characterized by the application of atomic energy and the appearance of computers. The fourth industrial revolution is taking place today in the information industry. As said above, people use different terms to describe it: "the fourth industrial revolution," "the fourth technological revolution," "the third wave," "an advance towards a society of science and technology," and "a transition to an information society." Despite its diverse names, one common feature is the wide application of new technologies, such as micro-electronics, genetic engineering, optical fibers, lasers, new materials, and new energy. This situation heralds changes in the traditional methods of production and the structure of industrial and social life. This trend is called the "new technological revolution" in China.

The coming of the new technological revolution and the emergence of new industries will have a profound impact on the structure of the national economy. A number of existing industries will decline, and some new industries will emerge and develop. Such a situation cannot but produce a profound influence on many countries and affect China's modernization drive as well. If we can make prompt use of the results of scientific and technological research to develop our economy and technology, we may be able to narrow the gap between us and the developed countries in these fields. Conversely, if we take the matter with indifference and fail to grasp this golden opportunity, the gap will widen.

To do so we must first proceed from the actual conditions of our country. China is a developing socialist country with low productivity. The emergence of new industries has offered us ample opportunities. If we can seize such opportunities and turn them to good account, we will be able to speed up our development and narrow our gap with the developed countries in the fields of economy and technology, catching up with or even outstripping them in a relatively short period of time. The worldwide new technological revolution also furnishes us with another opportunity. As the developed countries in the West are now concentrating their efforts on the development of new technologies and new products, some of the traditional industries, such as iron and steel, textile, shipbuilding, and automobile industries, are relegated to a state of "sunset industries." But the products of these industries are needed in all countries. We should take advantage of such a situation to develop these industries and push our way into the international market. Thus, we have to formulate a new strategy of industrial development and adopt the right industrial policy at the earliest date possible. This is of vital importance to the success or failure of our efforts to adapt ourselves to the new technological revolution and make the most of the results of advanced scientific and technological research to expedite our economic and technological development in the early stage of our modernization drive.

2. The reform in socialist countries

There is now a wave of reform and opening to the outside world in the socialist countries.

The socialist countries had practiced the centralization of economic policy decisions and a strict hierarchical administration in the past, which enforced the concentration of resources at crucial points of development, enabled economic growth to be pushed forward in the manner of campaigns and permitted the rapid transformation of the economic structure in the shape of industrialization based on the heavy industry and raw materials sectors. The success of this pattern in the past had impressed the whole world deeply, as pointed out by a Western historian, "From the point of view of global impact, it is likely that the Gosplan will prove to be of greater significance than the Communist International. The Five-Year Plans attracted worldwide attention, particularly because of the concurrent breakdown of the West's Economy. Socialism was no longer a dream of visionaries; it was a going concern.... Economic policies were influenced, consciously or unconsciously, by the Soviet success in setting priorities for the investment of national resources, which is the essence of planning." Yet when in the late 1950s and early 1960s the economic structure of the U.S.S.R. and other countries of Eastern Europe changed and became more mature and more complex, the efficacy of plan declined. The complexity of the economy increased more rapidly than did the capacity of the central economic administrative system to cope with this growing complexity in the planning process.

Since the mid-1950s, and more so in the 1960s, the weakness of the traditional socialist planning system were discussed with growing openness in Eastern Europe and the cry for reform was more widely heard. This wave of reform is accentuated through the rapid change of the technological regime. It is recognized by some leading scholars of the Eastern European countries and U.S.S.R. That reform is a necessity in order to overcome the structural crisis and to become competitive with the West. One leading Hungarian scholar pointed out, "All the major transitions from one technological regime to another—in the last third of the nineteenth century, in the first half of the twentieth century— created a structural crisis." One leading Soviet scholar also pointed out, "Why restructure? The old economic structure, the old economic policies, the management system and the old patterns of development did not correspond to the new conditions both inside the Soviet Union and internationally."

But we must understand that not only the socialist countries, but the world as a whole are facing changes of fundamental importance is becoming more distinct from year to year. Following revolutionary changes in technology and engineering, there is an urgent necessity in reorganization of the international economic relations. We also recognize the fact that science and technology is the engine for change, but not the driver. Hence, there is a necessity for coordinated development of social, economic and technological strategy and policies. This will form the basis of our vision of the future.

Since the Third Plenary Session of the 11th Central Committee of the Chinese Communist Party, China has achieved remarkable successes in economic reform. The reform which started from the rural areas in 1979 soon became an irreversible trend. The decision on the reform of the economic structure adopted by the Third Plenary Session of the Party's 12th Central Committee in 1984 set off an overall reform with stress laid on the cities. The decision marked a theoretical breakthrough in China's economic reform. It pointed out that our socialist economy is a planned commodity economy based on public ownership, which is an unavoidable stage in economic development.

3. The move of the center of world economy towards the Pacific

This trend involves the realignment of world economic relations and will lead to fiercer competition and a trial of strength in the worldwide economic war. It will bring opportunities and prosperity to China. At the same time, however, fierce competition coming along with it might compel us to become a supplier of raw materials and a market for other countries and thus widen our gap with them if we fail to increase our own economic strength. From this perspective, this trend poses a challenge to us as well.

Europe has been the strategic center of the world economy ever since World War II. For a long time, it has been the arena of contention between the United States and the Soviet Union. Since the mid-1970s, the economy of the region around the Pacific Ocean has developed rapidly at a growth rate nearly twice as high as that of Europe. The region has abundant raw materials, and its labor force and intellectual resources account for more than half of the world's total. Experts believe that the momentum of development of this region will be irreversibly higher than that of the areas around the Atlantic Ocean. By the time when the People's Republic of China celebrates its 100th anniversary, the region around the Pacific Ocean will be highly developed and will have become the focus of contention in the global economic war.

We must strive to become an economic power and play a leading role in the world arena by that time.

The three trends mentioned above provide us with both opportunities and challenges. It is imperative for us to seize the opportunities and meet the challenges. Moreover, we must not only catch up with the advanced countries but outstrip them; not only draw on foreign experience but create our own; not only maintain our international status but steadily raise it; and not only take up the challenge but take the initiative. Only then can we ensure our future prosperity.

Section 3
The Study of China's Development Strategy Enters a New Stage

The general task set by the 12th National Congress of the Chinese Communist Party is to unite the people of all our nationalities in working hard and self-reliantly to achieve, step by step, the modernization of our industry, agriculture, national defense and science and technology, and to make China a culturally advanced and highly democratic socialist country. To fulfill this historic task, it is necessary for us to make an in-depth study of our development strategy. It was against this background that research into China's development strategy flourished. Many regions, provinces, municipalities, and departments have conducted this work, achieved initial successes, and put it to good use.

Development strategy is the summation of the development goal and the policies, the measures and steps formulated for the realization of this goal. It is an overall, long-term, regular, key plan. An overall development strategy encompasses the systematic engineering of the whole society; it is not simply the sum total of the development strategies of various areas. Rather, it integrates organically the development strategies of various departments, regions, and trades. Coordinated development of the economy, science and technology, and the society as a whole is an objective law. Thus, strenuous efforts must be made by a country, a region, or a city to study the overall strategy for coordinated economic, social, scientific and technological development.

To formulate an appropriate development strategy, there must be correct guidelines, which are as follows:

(a) Formulate a development strategy that suits China's national conditions. In our socialist modernization, we must proceed from China's realities. We have to learn from the experience of foreign countries, but mechanical copying of the experience and models of other countries will get us nowhere. To build socialism with Chinese characteristics is the conclusion we have drawn by summing up the historical lessons over a long period of time.

The overall development strategy we are to formulate should have the following features: first, it should have Chinese characteristics instead of being a copy of the model of another country; second, it must be able to bring into full play the superiority of the socialist system and steadily improve it; and third, it must be designed to achieve rapid development and progress in realizing modernization.

(b) Make a comprehensive study of the strategies for economic, social, scientific, and technological development. Economic, social, scientific and technological developments affect and condition each other. Stressing one or two aspects to the neglect of the others will not achieve the purpose of development. Even if certain successes are made for the time being, they cannot last long.

A country' strategy for economic development is the basis and principal part of its overall development strategy. Great efforts must be made in this area. Meanwhile, economic development must rely on science and technology to gain new vitality. Diverse social factors such as historical development, cultural origin, national traditions, population, the cultural and educational level of the people, the social structure, and the management system all have close ties with economic, scientific, and technological development. Only by studying these factors comprehensively can we map out a satisfactory overall development strategy.

(c) Handle correctly the relations between growth rate and economic returns. In doing so, we should strive to achieve unity between growth rate and economic returns, giving priority to the improvement of economic returns. We must take this into account in formulating our development goal.

The development goal is formed of a complicated, multi-layer system of goals. The general goal is the summation of the entire goal system, which include the system of economic, social, scientific, technological, cultural, and environmental goals as well as the system of performance and growth rate goals. Under these is the system of sub-goals.

(d) Handle correctly the relations between immediate interests and long-term interests. In handling the relations between development speed and results and between accumulation and consumption and in considering the questions of scientific and technological advance, training of personnel, utilization of natural resources, population control, and environmental protection, we must not take into account our immediate interests at the expense of our long-term interests. In the exploitation and utilization of natural resources and in environmental protection and improvement, it is all the more necessary to integrate immediate and long-term interests. This principle must be consciously followed in working out the overall strategies.

(e) Pay attention to the study of the development of China's regional economy. China is a developing country with uneven economic development. Even in the developed regions, there are relatively underdeveloped localities. If the underdeveloped areas remain unchanged for a long time to come, they will play a restricting role in China's future development. Actually these regions and localities have many advantages and are areas where China's future lies. As the natural conditions, economic and technological levels, and social factors of various regions differ, the combination of various factors in these regions will show distinct features. Thus in formulating the development strategy of their own regions and carrying out the national development strategy, various regions must carry out the principle of suiting measures to local conditions, bringing the local advantages into full play, and adhering to rational distribution.

(f) Build a socialist civilization which is advanced materially as well as culturally and ideologically. After the stress of the work of the whole Party was shifted from economic construction to achieving modernization, the Party Central Committee has repeatedly declared that while building material civilization we must strive to build a socialist civilization with advanced culture and ideology. Material civilization is an indispensable basis for the building of a socialist society with advanced culture and ideology. A socialist civilization which is advanced culturally and ideologically gives great impetus to the building of civilization and ensures its correct development. We must attach great importance to this question in our study and include both aspects in mapping out our development strategy.

(g) Take into consideration the changes in the international environment. In formulating their development strategies, all countries have to give thought to the international environment surrounding them. This is particularly important to those countries carrying out the policy of opening to the world. That is why at the beginning of this book we made an estimate of the international environment. Because the international environment changes constantly, we have to analyze the present world situation and study the trends of political, economic, social, scientific, and technological developments in the world.

An overall strategy and development plan is being worked out by the departments concerned in China. Although the study of regional strategies has made much headway, its coordination with the overall strategy has just begun.

The study of China's development strategy has entered a new stage which is marked by the following characteristics:

—The study of the overall strategy is integrated with the study of sub-strategies;

—The study of regional development strategies has transcended regional administrative boundaries for joint inter-regional studies;

—The study of development strategy has been integrated

with efforts to meet the challenge of the worldwide new technological revolution;

—The study of development strategy has been linked up with the projection of who will play a leading role in the world in the twenty-first century;

—The study of development strategy has been combined with planning work instead of being merely the discussions of scholars;

—The study of development strategy has entered the stage of comprehensive study, shifting from qualitative study to an integration of qualitative and quantitative studies;

—The study of development strategy is now part of the exploration of the new model of the socialist planned commodity economy;

—The study of development strategy is connected with the economic restructuring;

—The study of development strategy is combined with the study of policy systems;

—The study of the development strategy is coupled with the improvement of the legal system and social security; and

—The study of development strategy is integrated with the study of the industrial development strategy, which is a major feature of the study.

Section 4
Changes in China's Economic Development Strategy

Beginning with the First Five-Year Plan (1953-57), we paid attention to viewing economic problems from the perspectives of the overall strategic situation and development prospects. However, as we lacked experience in building socialism at that time, we modeled some of our practices on those of the Soviet Union, later made some "left" mistakes in our guidelines, and failed in selecting the correct strategic goals for economic development, as well as the proper methods for achieving these goals.

At the Third Plenary Session of the 11th Central Committee

of the Chinese Communist Party, held towards the end of 1978, China decided to shift the focus of the work of the Party and state to socialist economic construction. At the same time, our country's economic development strategy also has began to change.

First, our strategic ideas changed. We gave up the practice of mechanically copying the models of other countries and decided to take a road of our own choice and build socialism with Chinese characteristics; we renounced product economy and natural economy and decided to develop a socialist planned commodity economy; we repudiated the "left" mistake of seeking quick success without regard to our abilities and decided to follow the principle of working hard and doing what we are capable of to achieve a steady, sustained, and coordinated development of our economy.

With the change in the guiding ideology, our choice of the goal for the country's economic development as well as the methods to realize this goal have also undergone a corresponding change.

1. The strategic goal has changed from concentrating on one sector only to paying attention to all-round development

In mapping out our development strategy in the past, we used to concentrate on economic development only. In this way we often neglected the interaction between various factors such as science and technology and people's lives. Beginning with the Sixth Five-Year Plan (1981-85), we changed the plan for the development of the national economy into a plan for socio-economic development, thus integrating economic development with social development. At the same time, we have stressed building a society with both material affluence and highly developed cultural and ideological standards, in the hope to enable the Chinese people to become well-educated, self-disciplined citizens with high ideals and moral integrity, and to build a socialist society with Chinese characteristics.

2. The focus of attention has changed from merely seeking a

certain economic growth rate and concentrating only on quantity to increasing economic returns and stressing quality, so that people can enjoy real benefits

The fundamental purpose of socialist economic construction is to meet the people's ever increasing material and cultural demands. This cannot be achieved by relying on quantity alone but requires improvement of quality and economic performance. The objective of quadrupling China's gross industrial and agricultural output value by the end of this century, set forth at the 12th Party Congress, is conditioned on increasing economic returns so that the people can have a relatively comfortable material and cultural life, a higher standard of living and a better quality of life. This embodies the unity of economic performance and growth rate, of quantity and quality, and of the development of production and the betterment of the people's standard of living. In this way we shall blaze a new trail in the development of our socialist economy which ensures a stable growth rate, better economic performance, improved quality, and more material benefits for the people.

3. A change has been made from merely stressing the key sector in isolation to stressing the role of the key sector to promote an all-round development so that the national economy can develop harmoniously

For a long time in the past, we one-sidedly stressed giving priority to the development of heavy industry to the neglect of agriculture and light industry. This resulted in the seriously disproportionate development of the various sectors of the national economy, while heavy industry itself failed to grow as anticipated. Today, our economic work is arranged on the basis of an overall analysis of the national economy, raising both the strategically key sectors to be developed and and the demand to establish a rational economic structure, so that the various social and economic departments and all fields of work can develop in coordination.

4. The way of expanding reproduction has changed from

building new enterprises to technologically revamping existing
enterprises

Ever since the founding of New China, we have built quite a
few new enterprises. This was entirely necessary to achieve our
industrialization. However, over a long period of time, our
development of production chiefly relied on the building of new
enterprises to the neglect of the technological upgrading of
existing enterprises. As a result, increasing numbers of capital
construction projects have been launched, and the construction
cycle has become longer and longer. As technological upgrading
was overlooked, a large number of enterprises have become
outdated in equipment, backward in technology, and low in
productivity. Beginning from the Seventh Five-Year Plan (1985-
90), China has laid the emphasis of capital construction on the
technological upgrading and renovation as well as expansion of
existing enterprises.

5. The unplanned population growth has been changed to family planning and greater attention has been given to the development of intellectual resources

The population problem is of vital importance to China's
social and economic development. People are the most important
element of the productive forces, but over-population puts heavy
pressure on economic growth. To turn population pressure into a
motive force, we have to carry out family planning and raise the
quality of men and women, which hinges on the development of
intellectual resources. As the quality of the people plays a decisive
role in the modernization drive, we take education and science as
one of the priorities of development. The decision on economic
restructuring adopted by the Party Central Committee called the
whole nation to respect knowledge and talented people and
considered it an important question for the country's
development.

6. The closed-door policy has been changed into a policy of actively opening to the outside world on the basis of independence and self-reliance

China's modernization can only be achieved by relying on our own strength. However, self-reliance was misconstrued in the past as self-sufficiency and the need to close our country to international exchanges, and this had produced a disastrous influence on our own development. After the Third Plenary Session of the 11th Party CentralCommittee, China set opening to the outside world as its long-term basic state policy. This will enable us to learn from the strong points of other countries to make up our deficiencies; to import foreign funds and technology and advanced management expertise to bring into fuller play China's own advantages; and to increase the competitiveness of Chinese products in the world market and create conditions for the export of Chinese technology and funds to other countries. This will facilitate the realization of our goal for modernization.

These changes are being made. Their progress depends on the reform of the economic structure; on the change from a closed, petrified economic model to an open economic model which will be full of vitality; on the shift from direct control to indirect control, which finds expression in the change from a mainly mandatory planned product economy to a mainly planned commodity economy; and on the switch from administrative means to economic means in economic management. These profound changes will involve redistribution of responsibilities and powers of the existing state administrative system, the manner of operation, the competence of government officials, and the adaptability of state organs to the changed socio-economic situation. In short, the changes in the national economic functions and the related political reform are very complex. This task is arduous, but the historical mission has to be accomplished. Through these changes, China will be able to blaze a new trail in its socialist economic construction and our country will create a new model of socialist modernization with Chinese characteristics. The ongoing changes will have a vital bearing on the country's future prosperity. We have to keep to the correct orientation. We are shaping our future.

CHAPTER II
PROSPECTS FOR CHINA'S DEVELOPMENT

Section 1
A Study of "China Towards the Year 2000"

1. How the study was initiated

After China walked out the decade-long turbulence of the "cultural revolution," the Third Plenary Session of the 11th Party Central Committee decided to shift the focus of work of the Party and government to the modernization drive. Since then, a series of guidelines for economic and social development were formulated and tremendous successes were achieved. Thus, the study of China's development up to the end of this century was put on the agenda. In 1981, leaders of the Party Central Committee and the State Council gave implicit instructions on the study of what China would like by the end of this century and what level would the material and cultural life of the Chinese people would reach then, hoping that through study and investigations a vivid and lively picture would be drawn to fire the enthusiasm of the people.

2. Purpose of the Study

The 12th National Congress of the Chinese Communist Party clearly set forth the strategic objectives, priorities, and steps required for China's socialist construction. In launching the study of "China Towards the Year 2000," it is our purpose to make a comprehensive study of China's economic, cultural, scientific, and technological developments, the people's standard of living, and the progress towards building a socialist society with advanced culture and ideology by the year 2000 and to get a clear, concrete picture of our development. This will be achieved through a comprehensive analysis of the domestic and international situation and subjective and objective conditions under the guidelines of the 12th Party Congress. At the same time, we shall explore all possible ways to achieve the strategic objectives of our socialist construction and select the optimum way to this end. Furthermore, we have to study the policies to be formulated to realize the goal and make predictive analyses of the results of the implementation of such policies. On the basis of these studies, we should work out the requirements for economic work at present and the measures to be adopted to facilitate the fulfillment of the grand strategic objectives set forth at the 12th Party Congress. In short, the study of "China Towards the Year 2000" is designed to better fulfill the strategic objectives pub forward by the 12th Party Congress by furnishing the Party Central Committee and the State Council with information based on scientific research, which can be used for making policy decisions and formulating policies; by providing the various regions and departments with reference materials that can be used for mapping out development plans for various undertakings; and by creating publicity of what China is to be like in the year 2000 to encourage the Chinese people to work hard for the fulfillment of the goal.

3. The method of study

The study of "China Towards the Year 2000" represents research into a large and complex socio-economic system. It is necessary to sum up the experience of the past, to take stock of the present, and to make forecasts for the future. Special attention should be paid to the study of coordinated economic and social developments to promote the building of a socialist civilization that is advanced culturally and ideologically as well as materially. We have to study projections of the development strategy and to make an analysis and exposition of clear and concrete scenarios. Obviously, it is a multi-level, interdisciplinary study that cuts across various departments. Thus, from the very beginning we made a systematic design of the contents, organization, and methods of study, and in the research work, we integrated the long-term goal with the present national conditions, long-term study with immediate study, and overall conceptual research with the study of concrete scenarios. In short, we combined theoretical research with practical study by seeking truth from facts. At the same time, we combined qualitative analysis and quantitative analysis, conventional and modern methods, in-depth survey and comprehensive research, and special research and coordinated study. Mutually complementary research methods were used throughout the study.

4. Results of the study

More than 400 specialists and scholars from over 100 scientific and technological institutions plunged themselves into the study of "China Towards the Year 2000" from various aspects. After more than two years of research they completed a main report and 12 sub-reports on population and employment, the economy, people's consumption, science and technology, education, natural resources, energy, the environment, agriculture, the transportation system, the international environment, and an overall quantitative analysis of China's economy towards the year 2000. At the same time, they compiled a "Summary of Data of Projections for China Towards the Year 2000." They also made in-depth studies and submitted special reports on China's public health, sports, communications, broadcasting and television, culture, society, oceanic development, building materials, and foreign trade. Detailed reports on railway, highway, water, ocean shipping, civil aviation, urban passenger, and pipeline transport were also written. Furthermore, a forecast study of various sectors and sub-sectors made by tens of thousands of specialists and scholars organized by the Chinese Science and Technology Association also yielded valuable results.

5. Evaluation of the research results

The publication of the study results by the State Council aroused warm responses throughout the country. The consensus of opinion was that this was the first high-level, comprehensive strategic study in China and that the results achieved were gratifying.

The study of "China Towards the Year 2000" made clear the few strategic goals for the country to choose as well as the possible policy decisions to be made and policies to be adopted to realize these goals. It represents a successful attempt to explore the road of socialist modernization with distinct Chinese characteristics as well as a strategic study of China's coordinated economic, social, scientific, and technological developments. It provides comprehensive reference materials for the country to make a long-term development strategy, draw up the five-year plans, enact current policies, and work out plans for the development of various regions, trades and undertakings. Many conclusive views and policy suggestions derived from the study have been adopted by the State Council.

The results achieved by the study are of important reference value to the work of various ministries and commissions. They are of the opinion that the study has made a systematic, all-round analysis of China's capabilities and potentials and were very helpful to their work.

The study of "China Towards the Year 2000" has accumulated useful experience for and fostered trans-departmental and interdisciplinary cooperation and exchange between national and social science workers, between theoretical and practical workers, and among economic departments, institutions of higher learning and scientific research institutes, which has resulted in the joint research of comprehensive projects by specialists from various industries, disciplines, and departments.

The study has aroused worldwide interest. Delegations from more than 40 countries have interviewed the research workers of this project. The TV stations of a number of countries reported on the study of "China Towards the Year 2000" under the title "China Advances Towards the Future." Major consultancy organizations of a number of countries have studied the brief introductions made public by China and translated them into various languages. "China Towards the Year 2000" and other relevant treatises were read at more than a dozen major international conferences. Interest in the project is steadily expanding.

Section 2
Population and Employment

China's population will be controlled to around 1.25 billion by the end of this century and employment will be diversified.

1. The size of the population will be put under control and the growth rate will be slowed down

Before the founding of New China in 1949, the country's population situation was described as "a high rate of birth and death, and a low rate of natural increase." In 1936, the birth rate was 38 per thousand, the death rate 28 per thousand, and the rate of increase 10 per thousand. The average life span then was only 30-35 years. During the 109 years from 1840 to 1949, China's population rose from 412 million to 512 million, with an annual growth rate of less than 1 percent.

From 1949 to the beginning of the 1970s, the growth of China's population entered a period of rapid increase following the development of the economy, the rise of the people's standard of living and the popularization of medical and sanitary services. Population reproduction for this period changed to one of "high birth rate, low death rate, and a high rate of natural increase." In 1970, the birth rate was 33.4 per thousand, the death rate 7.6 per thousand, and the rate of natural increase 25.83 per thousand. The national census in 1975 showed the country's population to be 919.7 million, with an annual growth rate exceeding 20 per thousand. The unprecedented rate of population growth brought tremendous difficulties to the state in such matters as increasing the accumulation of funds, accelerating the development of the economy, raising the people's standard of living, providing employment, developing education, and protecting the ecological environment. For instance, the output of grain increased by 61 percent from 1959 to 1980, but 48 percent of it was used to meet the needs of the newly added population, so only 13 percent could go to bettering the people's lives.

To change this situation and enable population growth to keep pace with socio-economic development, the government adopted a variety of policies and measures for birth control. With the implementation of family planning since early 1970s, the birth rate has fallen dramatically. In 1976, it fell below 20 per thousand for the first time. The rate of natural increase also dropped from 25.8 per thousand in 1970 to 11.23 per thousand in 1985.

The third national census conducted in 1982 showed the population of the country's 29 provinces, municipalities, and autonomous regions (not including Taiwan) to be 1.008 billion. Population growth during the period from 1983 to 2000 is projected as follows:

—Low projection: The total population will be 1.204 billion with an average annual growth rate of 9.5 per thousand;

—Medium projection: The total population will be 1.248 billion with an average annual growth rate of 11.5 per thousand;

—High projection: The total population will be 1.280 billion with an average annual growth rate of 13.4 per thousand.

These projections indicate that China's population by the year 2000 will exceed the present figure by at least 200 million, but the rate of natural increase is gradually declining. According to the medium projection, the natural growth rate of 13 per thousand in the late 1980s would fall to 12 per thousand at the beginning, 10 per thousand in the middle, and 8 per thousand at the end of the 1990s. According to such growth rates, the country's population will be 1.119 billion in 1990, 1.191 billion in 1995 and 1.248 billion in 2000. By the end of this century, the world population will reach 6.3 billion. In line with the medium projection, which is more likely to be realized, the proportion of China's population to that of the world total will be 19.8 percent, or about one-fifth.

2. Infant mortality rate will fall and life expectancy will rise

The physical condition of the Chinese people has improved rapidly in the last 30 years or so. With further improvement of medical and sanitary services and continuous improvement of the living standards, the rate of infant mortality is expected to drop to 20 per thousand by 2000 from 35 per thousand in 1981. The people's life expectancy will climb to 72 years in 2000 from 68 years in 1982.

3. The population pattern will change from the young to the adult and then towards the aging

The age structure of China's population belongs to the young (the pattern of growth); at present, its median is 22.9 years. According to the medium projection, however, by the year 2000 the proportion of people aged 0-14 years will drop, while that of those aged 15-64 years and that of above 65 will rise (see Table 2-1), thereby turning the age structure into an adult (or stable) pattern. The respective proportions of the three age groups will change from 33.6 percent, 61.4 percent, and 4.91 percent in 1982 to 24.3 percent, 68.8 percent, and 6.9 percent in 2000, with the median age of the population being 32 years. The problems arising from a relative aging of the population should arouse our attention as the problem will become outstanding in the twenty-first century.

Table 2-1

CHANGE IN AGE STRUCTURE OF CHINA'S
POPULATION FROM 1985 TO 2000
(medium projection)

Year	Total Population (million)	Years of Age		
		1-14 (%)	15-64 (%)	65 & above (%)
1985	1,050	30.0	65.0	5.0
1990	1,119	26.0	58.4	5.6
1995	1,191	25.2	68.6	6.2
2000	1,248	24.8	68.8	6.9

4. The trend of urbanization will accelerate

In 1982, China had an urban population of 210 million, which accounted for 21.2 percent of the national total. This proportion is not only much lower than that of the developed countries (72 percent), but also lower than that of many developing countries. Along with the progress of economic reform in the cities and the rapid development of the rural economy, it will an inevitable trend that the rural population will move into cities and towns. According to the medium projection, the proportion of China's urban population will increase to 38 percent (467 million) of the total. This means that the ratio of urban to rural population will be almost 4:6, about the average world level at present.

Moreover, the proportion of people living in major and medium-sized cities in the total urban population will decrease drastically from 70 percent in 1982 to 44.1 percent by 2000, whereas that of people living in small towns (each with a population of 100,000) will gradually increase from 30 percent to 55.9 percent in the same period. In other words, the rural population will concentrate in rural towns instead of flowing into big and medium-sized cities. This may be said as a special feature of China's urbanization.

It is estimated that the number of cities will increase considerably. There were 245 cities in China in 1982 which will increase to 375 by 2000. Among these, the number of cities with a urban population exceeding 1 million will increase from 10 to 31 and small cities with a population of 100,000-200,000 each will jump to 226 from 126.

The regional distribution of population will become more rational. Yet, no fundamental change is expected in the situation that the population density in the east is greater than in the west.

5. The working-age population will grow faster than the total population and the number of employed people will increase as never before

By the year 2000, China's working-age population will increase to 858 million from 621 million in 1982, a net increase of 237 million. Such rapid growth is unprecedented.

A rising employment rate for the total population and a declining employment rate for the working-age population is an inevitable trend in the course of modernization in developing countries. The former is affected by the age structure of the population and the latter by the increasing number of educated people among the working-age population. It is estimated that the employment rate of China's total population will rise to 52.7 percent by 2000 from 44.0 percent in 1982, while that of the working-age population will fall from 80 percent to 75 percent in the same period, which is about the general level of the developed countries at present.

6. Two trends in the flow of the labor force

The first trend is the transfer of the agricultural labor force to township industry and commerce. Usually, the newly added labor force in China every year has mainly been absorbed by agriculture. The state of affairs will change with the advance of the modernization drive and the urbanization of the population. A vast number of agricultural workers will switch to township industry and commerce. It is estimated that the proportion of people engaged in agricultural production to the total labor force will fall to 51 percent from more than 72 percent in 1982.

The second trend pertains to the transfer of the labor force from material production departments to non-material production departments. The proportion of the newly-increased labor force engaged in non-material production departments will gradually increase, and a part of the labor force currently engaged in material production departments will turn to tertiary industries. There is one forecast that the ratio between the labor force in material production departments and that in non-material production departments will change from 1:0.14 in 1982 to 1:0.34 in 2000, while the number of people engaged in tertiary industries will grow from 54 million to 165 million. If these projectioned targets can be reached, it will be tantamount to making a major step towards turning the pressure of population and employment into a motive force.

Section 3
Economic Strength

1. China's economic strength has increased enormously

Taking into consideration various factors such as economic performance, economic structure, growth rate, and improvement of the people's standard of living, we have worked out a variety of schemes forecasting China's overall economic capability by the year 2000. The forecast shows that the optimum scheme is one which has an accumulation rate of 29 percent and an energy elastic coefficient (the ratio between energy growth rate and economic growth rate) of 0.85. According to this scheme, the data for the main economic indexes by the year 2000 are as follows.

The gross annual output value of industry and agriculture will reach 2,953 billion yuan, 4.1 times the 720.7 billion yuan in 1980, with an annual growth rate of 7.3 percent.

GNP will reach 1,184 billion U.S. dollars, 4.4 times that of 1980, with an average annual growth rate of 7.7 percent. Calculated in terms of a population of 1.25 billion at that time, the per-capita GNP will be 945 U.S. dollars. This will meet the requirement set forth by Deng Xiaoping that the per-capita GNP of the Chinese will reach 800-1,000 U.S. dollars by the end of this century.

The national income will reach 1,450 billion yuan, 3.9 times the 368.8 billion yuan of 1980, with an average annual growth rate of 7.1 percent and an average per-capita national income of 1,161.8 yuan. All the above figures are calculated in terms of the constant prices of 1980.

According to calculations made by the World Bank, China's GNP in 1980 was 283.2 billion U.S. dollars, accounting for only 2.4 percent of the world's total. Among the 159 countries it listed, China took the eighth place behind the United States, the Soviet Union, Japan, the Federal Republic of Germany, France, Britain, and Italy. Forecasts of the economic development of various countries show that by 2000 China will overtake Italy and Britain to take the sixth place or may even outstrip France to rank the fifth. One forecast indicates that China may possibly surpass the Federal Republic of Germany to take the fourth place.

Judging by its total economic strength, China can be called an economic power, but given its large population, its per-capita GNP will still be very low. Of the 159 countries listed by the World Bank, China's per-capita GNP was 290 U.S. dollars in 1980, which ranked it 133rd. It is estimated that China will still rank below the 80th place by the year 2000 and will therefore remain a country with a lower-middle income. As the report to the 13th National Congress of the Chinese Communist Party pointed out, "Ever since the Third Plenary Session of the 11th Party Central Committee, we have been carrying out a strategic plan for economic development. This plan involves three steps. The first step is to double the GNP of 1980 and solve the problem of food and clothing for our people. This task has been largely fulfilled. The second step is to double it again by the end of this century, thus enabling our people to lead a fairly comfortable life. The third step is by the middle of the next century to reach the per-capita GNP level of moderately developed countries. This will mean that modernization has been basically accomplished and that our people have begun to enjoy a relatively affluent life. Then, on this basis, China will continue to advance." Thus we have to traverse a long and rugged road before we can take our place among the advanced countries in the world.

2. The industrial setup is becoming rationalized

In 1980, the Chinese people's per-capita GNP was 290 U.S. dollars; it is expected to increase to 954 U.S. dollars by the year 2000. In other words, China will be in a period of transition from a low-income country to a middle-income country. International experience indicates that this will be a period in which the industrial setup will undertake remarkable changes and the process of industrialization will be speeded up. To meet the needs of changing consumption patterns and the establishment of more harmonious economic relations, it will be necessary to constantly readjust the industrial structure and increase economic returns in order to achieve a basic balance between the general supply and general demand.

Up to the end of this century, the ratios between China's

agriculture and industry, newly-emerging industries and traditional industries, mining industries and processing industries, production departments and infrastructure facilities, and the primary, secondary and tertiary industries will be constantly readjusted to achieve rationalization and modernization. The modernization of the economic structure will be dealt with at length in Chapter IV.

3. The distribution of the productive forces will improve considerably

In the 1980s, China strives to make full use of the existing enterprises and bases in the eastern part of the country and steadily promote their modernization. Starting in the 1990s and continuing after the year 2000, the focus of attention will be gradually shifted to developing the central and western regions while making continued efforts to develop the old industrial bases in the east and the coastal open cities.

The eastern region will concentrate its efforts on developing those processing industries which consume less energy and raw materials, cause little or no pollution, and are technologically sophisticated, produce goods that are competitive in the world market, and turn out high-tech, precision, sophisticated new products. Processing industries for local agricultural and sideline products and the crude processing for mineral products will be diverted to raw material producing areas and energy-rich areas in the central and western regions. Coastal open cities will strive to improve their infrastructure facilities and create favorable investment environments to speed up the import of foreign funds and advanced technology.

The central inland region will focus on developing the coal and heavy chemical industrial base with Shanxi Province as the center (including northern Shaanxi Province, western Henan Province, the western part of Inner Mongolia, and part of the Ningxia Hui Autonomous Region). Strenuous efforts will be made to develop metallurgical, coal, and chemical industries. Stress will be put on promoting shipping on the Yangtze River and building the Yangtze River water conservancy projects. A comprehensive industrial belt will be built step by step along the Yangtze. Industries in the inland areas will be readjusted and reorganized to improve their economic performance.

Preparations will also be made for the large-scale development of the western region. This not only requires material preparations but also the training of various kinds of personnel so as to keep pace with the advance in scientific and technological research as well as the development of management. Attention must be paid to geological surveys, to the development of industries that can bring into full play the local advantages, and to speeding up the construction of transport and other infrastructure facilities, especially inter-regional main lines of transport.

4. The industrial output value will be increased to the level of the United States in the early 1980s

By 2000, China's industrial output value is expected to reach 2,420 million yuan (including that of rural industries), about 4.7 times that of the 519.4 billion yuan of 1980. This roughly amounts to the industrial output value of the United States in the yearly 1980s.

Section 4
Energy

1. The energy situation is improving, power shortages remain acute

Since the Third Plenary Session of the 11th Party Central Committee, a series of major steps have been taken to readjust the energy policy, speed up the development of the energy industry, conserve energy, and remarkable successes have been achieved. The supply of energy has improved enormously. However, the contradictions between energy supply and demand have not been solved fundamentally. This situation is particularly serious in the supply of electricity, of which there is a shortage of some 50 million kwh. About one-quarter of industrial capacity has not been brought into full play as a result of power shortages. With the high rate of growth of the national economy, power shortages seem to be increasing.

Remarkable successes have been scored in solving energy shortages in the rural areas since the implementation of a policy aimed at making comprehensive use of a variety of energy resources available in the countryside. However, there is still an acute shortage of energy, especially energy for agricultural production and township industries. Today 300 million rural people still have no access to electricity; 85 percent of the fuel consumed by 800 million rural people in their daily life comes from non-commodity sources. This means that 180 million tons of firewood and 230 million tons of plant stalks are consumed every year, and there is still a 20 percent shortage. This is one of the main reasons for the wanton felling of trees, the resulting water and soil erosion, and the worsening of the ecological environment.

2. Make domestically produced energy the basis of economic and social life

China has rich and varied energy resources, but they are unevenly distributed, and the average per-capita share is small. The country's economic and social life is based on domestically produced energy and imported energy accounts for a small proportion of the total consumed. This situation will continue till the end of this century. China is one of the few countries in the world which relies on coal as fuel. The energy consumption pattern will be improved somewhat in the future, with the development of hydroelectric power, nuclear energy, and natural gas, which will help reduce the consumption of coal to a certain degree. But, the situation in which coal is used as the major fuel will not see fundamental change. As the energy demand increases sharply in the rural areas, we must develop technology to tap the potential of small-scale energy resources available in these localities, while continuing the efforts to increase the supply of commodity energy. Although our per-capita energy consumption is very low, China is nevertheless the third largest energy consuming country in the world. Our energy consumption for per unit output value is very high, and the waste of energy is a serious problem. We must make ceaseless efforts to tap our potential for energy conservation and reduce energy consumption.

3. The contradictions between energy demand and supply have to be tackled by the means of science and technology

In regard to China's energy demands by the year 2000, experts have forecast two scenarios. The first puts the total energy requirement at 1.56 billion tons of standard coal. This estimate is based on the demand that industrial and agricultural output value quadrupled and that the people be enabled to lead a relatively comfortable life, as well as such factors as changes in economic structure, technological progress, and energy conservation. The second puts the energy requirement at 1.7 billion tons of standard coal. This figure is derived by supposing the elastic coefficient of energy consumption to be 1, or in other words, that energy demand in 2000 will be 2.4 billion tons of standard coal, or twice as much as that of 1980. From this figure is deducted out 300 million tons of standard coal which will be conserved through technological improvement and 400 million tons of standard coal conserved through structural reform.

There are also two forecast schemes for energy supply in 2000. The low projection is 1.3 billion tons of standard coal, and the high projection is 1.48 billion tons of standard coal. According to these forecasts, the largest difference between supply and demand is 400 million tons of standard coal, the smallest difference 80 million tons of standard coal. This difference should be eliminated by speeding up technological progress and reducing energy consumption.

4. There will be marked changes in the regional distribution of energy supply and demand

The general tendency is that the stress of energy development will move westward and shortages in energy supply in the east will be more acute. It is estimated that by 2000 the increased coal output of Shanxi and Inner Mongolia will account for two-thirds of that of the whole country. Shanxi Province will ship out 300 million tons of coal. Thus, the transport of Shanxi coal to other areas is a problem of overall importance. The focus of the oil industry in this century will remain in the eastern part of the country, and the hope of future exploration lies in the west and offshore areas. The proportion of oil processing in the northeast will be gradually reduced and that in the central-south and southwest will be gradually increased. By the turn of this century, seven regional power grids will take shape. Of these, the central, southwest, and south China power grids will be basically self-sufficient; the northeast and east China power grids will be in short supply and huge amounts of thermo-power and hydro-power will be sent to the two regions from north and central China by means of long-distance, super high-tension wires. Meanwhile, efforts will be made to develop nuclear power.

5. Energy development technology will be greatly updated

By the end of this century, the technological level of energy development and utilization, the technological level in the development of energy equipment as well as the ability to develop energy technology self-reliantly will reach the levels the developed countries had reached in the late 1970s and   early 1980s and will surpass those levels in some respects.

Section 5
Natural Resources

1. Natural resources are unevenly distributed over a vast area

China is divided into seven zones with different climate conditions from north to south. Mountainous areas account for two-thirds of the country's territory. The distribution of water resources is extremely uneven, with 80 percent being concentrated in the Yangtze River valley and areas south of the river. Mineral resources are also unevenly distributed. Iron ore resources are concentrated in the Liaodong Peninsula, eastern Hebei Province, the area to the west of Panzhihua in Sichuan Province, and along the lower and middle reaches of the Yangtze River. The practice of shipping coal from north China to the south and shipping phosphorus from the south to the north will continue for a long time to come.

2. While the country's total amount of natural resources is huge, the per-capita share is small

China's reserves of hydroelectric power resources amount to 680 million kwh, which ranks first in the world. The potential value of 45 kinds of minerals are estimated at 11,000 billion U.S. dollars, ranking third in the world. But, its per-capita share of most natural resources is lower than the world average. For instance, although the verified reserves of 25 minerals—manganese, bauxite, lead, zinc, cobalt, tungsten, tin, molybdenum, antimony, mercury, bismuth, copper, tantalum, niobium, lithium, rare earth, coal, fluorite, magnesite, phosphorus, sulfur, barite, asbestos, gypsum, and graphite—all rank among the five largest in the world, the per-capita share of quite a few of them is lower than that of many developing countries, thus requiring that we use natural resources economically in developing our economy.

3. There are great potentials in the comprehensive exploitation and utilization of natural resources

China has about 268 million hectares of land suitable for afforestation, 3.3 times that of the existing afforested land. It has over 1.3 hectares of beach land and shallow waters along the coast and only 14 percent of this is being used. In addition, there are huge potentials for offshore oil exploitation. Mineral deposits are characterized by their intergrowth and complex composition, and there is much room for their comprehensive utilization.

4. Ground resources are in short supply and attention should be paid to increasing production and practicing economy

Under the pressure caused by population growth, there will continue to be a strain on ground resources in the next 20 years. by the turn of this century, China's per-capita share of cultivated land will be reduced to 0.1 hectare. Increasing production by applying scientific methods is necessary in order to attain the planned output targets for agricultural products. The country's total water resources are insufficient. In the Liaohe River valley, the lower reaches of the Yellow River, the coastal areas of Shandong Province in north China, where cities, factories, and mines are concentrated, as well as in the arid areas of northwest China, the difficulties will remain a problem to be solved over a long period of time. The situation in which the demand for timber surpasses its growth can be improved only after a long period of hard work. China's forest coverage accounts for only 12 percent of its land area. If 90 percent of the 268 million hectares of land suitable for afforestation were planted with trees, and 630,000 hectares of shelter belts were built for pastureland, highways, and shorelines, the country's forest coverage could reach 26 percent.

5. Minerals resources can be basically self-sufficient

There are many areas in the country where mineral resources are yet to be exploited. These resources can meet our demand for the production of 94 million tons of steel, 5.1 million tons of ten nonferrous metals, 64 million tons of nitrogenous, phosphate, and potash fertilizers, and 300 million tons of cement. Other mineral resources can be basically self-sufficient, and some can have surpluses. Only a few minerals such chromium, potassium, and diamonds have inadequate reserves.

6. There are broad prospects for the development of marine resources

Sea fishing, sea water salt production, ocean shipping, marine aquatic products breeding, and other traditional marine industries have enormous potentials, and their modernization is urgently needed. Many new areas of marine resources development such as deep-sea oil exploration, marine chemical industries, and seabed metal exploitation are still in the initial stage. The vast seas will be an important source from which China can extract natural resources. Preliminary forecasts show that in the development of marine resources, offshore oil exploitation will develop the fastest in this century. If it's development is normal, China's offshore oil output should reach 70 million tons by the end of this century.

Section 6
Agriculture

China's agriculture will develop in breadth and depth in the years to come. Forecasts show that our agricultural production has a bright future. With hard work we will build a modernized agriculture, prosperous towns, and affluent villages by the end of this century.

1. Agricultural production will increase steadily; agriculture, forestry, animal husbandry, sideline production, and fishery will develop in coordination

According to forecasts, between now and the end of this century, the gross agricultural output value (including the output value of township industries and industries run by rural villages) will grow at an average annual rate of 7.7 percent, and agricultural output value (including that of crop cultivation, forestry, animal husbandry, sideline production, and fishery) will grow at an average annual rate of 5.2 percent. The development of crop cultivation, forestry, animal husbandry, sideline production and fishery will be coordinated. The output of various kinds of farm and sideline products will increase steadily, their quality will improve, and the percentage of marketable products will rise continuously. At the same time, food processing, feed processing, building and building materials industries, catering and service trades, and other forms of cooperative industries and private enterprises will develop in the rural areas to invigorate the commodity economy and better meet the needs of the people in the towns and the countryside.

2. The per-capita share of major farm products will increase by wide margins

By the end of this century, the country's annual grain output is expected to increase to 520-535 million tons; cotton to 5.1-5.25 million tons; oil-bearing crops to 21.3-21.8 million tons; meat to

27.8-30 million tons, eggs to 10.2-16 million tons; milk to 28.8-36 million tons; and aquatic products to 11 million tons. Calculated in terms of a population of 1.248 billion, the per-capita share of grain will be 415-429 kilograms; vegetable oil and sugar, 6-6.25 kilograms; meat, 22.5-24 kilograms; eggs, 8- 12.5 kilograms; milk, 23.29 kilograms; and aquatic products, 9 kilograms. The per-capita consumption of fruit and vegetables will also increase. These represent a considerable rise over the 1983 national averages of per-capita consumption: grain, 232.3 kilograms; edible oil, 4.25 kilograms; meat, 12.35 kilograms; eggs, 2.96 kilograms; and sugar, 4.47 kilograms.

3. The structure of agriculture and the exploitation of natural resources will gradually become rationalized

The structure of China's agricultural production will undergo a series of changes by the end of this century. The proportion of the output value of crop farming in the total agricultural output value will drop markedly while that of forestry, animal husbandry, sideline production, and fishery will increase. As compared with 1980, the output value of crop farming will fall to 53.5 percent from 71.7 percent, while that of forestry will increase to 8.7 percent from 4.8 percent; animal husbandry to 27.7 percent from 17.2 percent, sideline production to 7.4 percent from 4.4 percent, and fishery to 2.8 percent from 2.0 percent.

The newly established rural industries will expand much faster than traditional agriculture, forestry, animal husbandry, sideline production, and fishery. By 2,000, the output value of rural industries will increase to 46.5 percent from 21.7 percent in 1980. In regards to crop farming, the growth of feed and cash crops will be faster than that of grain crops. The degree of intensive farming will be heightened considerably.

It is estimated that by the end of this century, the proportions of food crops, cash crops, and other crops in the total area sown to crops will be 74 percent, 15 percent, and 11 percent, respectively. Forest coverage will reach 20 percent, and annual timber output will exceed 100 million cubic meters. The output of meat of grasslands will reach 1.2 million tons, a three-fold increase over the present level, but most of the meat consumed in the country will continue to come from farming areas. The output of aquatic products will be double the present figure.

Section 7
Transport

Transport is part of the infrastructure of the national economy, and so far it has been a weak link in our country's economic development. China's transport services will develop by leaps and bounds up to the end of this century, but even then it will not fully meet the demand.

1. The demand for transport will keep on rising

According to forecasts, passenger transport will expand continuously at a high rate, and the growth of passenger transport by highway and civil aviation will be greater than that of railway and water transport. The volume of passenger transport by 2000 will be 5.3-5.9 times that of 1980; the rotation volume of passenger transport will be 4-4.5 times the figure of 1980. The growth rate in the volume of freight transport will be slightly lower than that of the gross industrial and agricultural output value. The volume of freight transport in 2000 will be 2.9-3.1 times that of 1980; the rotation volume of freight transport will increase 3.6-3.7 times. The handling capacity of coastal harbors will also increase rapidly.

2. Transport can meet the demand of development (the first prospect forecast)

Strenuous efforts should be made to enable transport to meet the basic needs of national economic development and social development before 1990 and pave the way for vigorous economic growth in the following decade. By 2000, transport should fully meet the needs of economic and social development and really become a pioneer in economic growth. To this end, it is necessary to build 30,000-40,000 kilometers of new railways. This will bring the country's total mileage of railways to 80,000-90,000 kilometers, of which 25-30 percent will be double-tracked. In addition, all the locomotives will be modernized. The mileage of highways will reach 1.5-2 million kilometers, of which 100,000 kilometers will be first-grade or second-grade highways. The number of harbor berths will reach 1,000, of which 700 will be deep-water ones. Ten thousand-ton class ships will be able to sail on 10,000 kilometers of inland rivers. The total investment for all this will exceed 500 billion yuan (calculated in terms of 1980 constant prices).

3. Transport basically meets the needs of development (the second prospect forecast)

The strain on transport industry will be somewhat eased before 1990. By 2,000, transport will basically meet the needs of national economic and social development. To translate this prognosis into reality, it is necessary to build 18,000-23,000 kilometers of new railways to bring railway mileage up to 70,000-75,000 kilometers, of which 24 percent will be double-tracked. The mileage of railways on which diesel and electric locomotives can operate will amount to 80 percent of the country's total. About 400,000-600,000 kilometers of new highways will be built to bring the national total highway mileage to 1.3-1.5 million kilometers, of which 60,000 kilometers will be first-grade and second-grade highways. There will be 550-600 deep-water berths at coastal harbors. Civil air routes will extend to 400,000-450,000 kilometers. Pipeline transport will cover 30,000-35,000 kilometers. The total transport network will extend for 1.988- 2.168 million kilometers. To accomplish these tasks, a total investment of 350-380 billion yuan is required.

4. Transport remains strained even at the end of this century which impedes development (the third prospect forecast)

Strains on transport will continue till 1990 and the situation will become worse by 2000. Transport remains the outstanding hindrance to the national economic and social development.

Of the three prospects forecast, efforts should be made to strive to turn the first prospect into reality. But there are tremendous difficulties in doing so. The third prospect should be avoided by all means. We must go all out to ensure the realization of the second.

5. A comprehensive transport system with rational structure will be built

All manners of transport in China will develop under the guidance of an overall plan for a comprehensive transport network. Attention must be given to coordinated development and rational utilization of all types of transport. A crisscrossing, comprehensive network of transport will be built and it will embrace railway, water, highway, civil aviation, and pipeline transport and be based on railway trunk lines, major highways, ocean shipping, shipping on the Yangtze River, the Pearl River, and the Grand Canal as well as oil and gas pipelines. The economic returns of the transport system will be increased enormously, and the distribution of the transport network and the pattern of transport will be rationalized.

Section 8
Ecological Environment

1. Destruction of the environment will be somewhat eased and in certain aspects will be brought under control and improve

In the years up to the end of this century, the areas suffering from water and soil erosion will be gradually reduced. The area of alkalinized land will shrink, and by the year 2000, more than 3.3 million hectares of such land will be ameliorated. By the end of this century, forested areas will exceed 168 million hectares, with forest coverage reaching about 18 percent.

2. Pollution of agricultural environment could aggravate, but the damage caused by certain kinds of pollution can be removed

The area of cultivated land suffering from the three industrial wastes (waste gas, waste water, and industrial residue) is likely to expand. The total amount of industrial residue will possibly double by the end of this century, while the loss of nitrogenous fertilizer caused by soil erosion will increase. But with the cessation of the production and use of "666" and "DDT," pollution caused by certain pesticides can be eliminated.

3. Urban industrial pollution will be brought under control, and city environment will improve

With an enhanced capacity to harness rivers, water pollution will be lessened, the quality of ground water in key areas will be much improved, and the damage caused by ground water to farmland, crops, and fishery will be brought under control. The total amount of dust emission will be reduced. The average density of sulfur dioxide discharge in southern cities will be below the second-class standard, while northern cities may reach the second-class standard. Acid rain pollution may increase.

The comprehensive utilization rate of solid wastes will be raised to 45 percent from the present 25 percent, and the amount of their disposal will come to 500 million tons. The rate of treatment of toxic wastes will reach 70 percent.

4. The damage caused by environmental pollution to the people's health will lessen

By the end of this century, pollution of the atmosphere will be somewhat reduced. The spread of epidemic diseases with water as the medium will be brought under control. The problem of polluted drinking water will be solved for 150 million people. The environment and hygienic conditions in towns and the countryside will be improved generally. Owing to the improvement of environment and other factors, life expectancy will reach 72 years.

Section 9
Education

1. An educational system which is geared to the needs of modernization, the world, and the future has taken shape

Economic development and the people's desire to get prosperous push education in the direction of meeting the needs of economic and social development. To better do business with Chinese and foreign customers, enterprises will strive for higher efficiency and better economic returns. Competition between enterprises will ever more clearly find expression in competition between skilled people and the quality of their labor force. The trend in education will change as the reform deepens. The pursuit of diploma will be replaced by more attention to practical skills. Attention to pre-employment education will be coupled with continued education after employment. Instead of relying mainly on state planning, the training of specialized personnel will chiefly depend on the law of demand and supply. The guiding ideology for education will shift from purely passing on knowledge to attaching greater importance to the development of intellectual resources and the training of the students' practical abilities. A new situation will emerge in which knowledge and skilled people are respected, education becomes the concern of all people and is geared to the needs of the modernization drive, and the promotion of education is coordinated with economic and social development.

2. The needs for specialized personnel will be met

From 1949 to 1985, China's educational institutions trained a total of 4.72 million college graduates, 8.03 million vocational secondary school graduates, 66.72 million senior high school graduates, 208.06 junior high school graduates, and 426.43 million primary school graduates. During this period the number of institutions of higher learning increased from 205 in 1949 to 1,016 in 1985, and the total enrollment of undergraduate students increased from 116,504 to 1,703,115, or a 14.5-fold increase. Graduate education had a very modest beginning during the early 1950s. In 1978, there was a turn in the tide with an enrollment of 10,708 graduate students that year, and there has been a spectacular expansion of the graduate education program since then. The total enrollment of graduate students, including those in research institutes, grew from 21,604 in 1980 to 87,331 in 1985, an increase of 32.2 percent annually. Despite such increases, however, the training of specialized personnel is far from adequate in meeting the demands of the national economy for professionals.

Forecasts by various departments show that by the year 2000 there will be a total demand for 49 million specialized personnel, 3.5 times the number available by June 1983. Of this, 12 million will be college graduates and above, 5.5 times the number available currently. In view of this demand, it is estimated that an aggregate number of some 40 million specialized personnel should be trained in the 18 years between 1983 and 2000. Of these, graduate students will number 770,000, college graduates, 20 million, and students of secondary vocational schools about 20 million. According to forecast, the discipline pattern of the specialized personnel will change markedly. The proportion of personnel in the fields of management, finance, political science, and law will go up, while the numbers of those in the field of engineering will drop. The above demand is based on the existing personnel system. With the advance of the economic structural reform, the personnel system will become rationalized, efficiency will increase, and the actual need for specialized personnel will be less than the number put forward by the employing units. Study shows that a realistic target of the aggregate number of specialized personnel to be trained in the 18 years between 1983 and 2000 is 34.4 million people. Of this, the number of graduate students will be 700,000, college graduates, 8.7 million, special course college students, 8 million, and secondary vocational school graduates, 17 million. The number of college students to be trained in the 18 years is more than four times that of the national total in June 1983.

3. The foundation of basic education will become more consolidated

The students now studying in universities, high schools, and primary schools will become the backbone of the work force active in all fields in the twenty-first century. Accordingly, it is necessary to strengthen basic education now. By the end of this century, secondary and primary schools in most parts of the country will be equipped with necessary laboratory equipment, music, sports, and fine arts teaching instruments, and audio-visual aids. The equipment of some schools will approach the international level of the 1980s.

According to the forecast, by the year 2000 the proportion of enrollment of rural primary school graduates in junior high schools will increase from the present 64 percent to about 95 percent (in cities it is now around 98 percent). About 90 percent of the junior high school graduates will be up to the required standard. A nine-year compulsory education program will be introduced throughout the country. This is about the present level of the developed countries and will surpass the level of other developing countries in 2000. All forms of senior high school education will be developed, and vocational senior school education will expand considerably.

4. Professional technical education and secondary vocational education will develop noticeably

By the end of this century, all young people will have to go through regular or part-time professional education and professional training before they are assigned jobs. A professional training system will be set up and perfected so that young people can receive training in labor skills and professional ethics before and after they are employed.

According to forecasts, the demand for secondary vocational school graduates by all trades and professions will at least double the total number of secondary vocational school graduates trained in the 35 years from 1949 to 1985. With the reform in the teaching system and the methods and contents of teaching, the development of the secondary vocational education can meet this demand.

5. A multi-strata, efficient higher educational network will take shape

It is estimated that by the end of this century, higher education will continue to be based chiefly on full-time day school education, while in-service higher education will be based mainly on evening universities, correspondence courses (including through radio and TV broadcasts) and college education received through self-study and passing examinations for all required courses. By 2000 the number of students enrolled in all institutions of higher learning will reach 6-7 million, ranking China third or fourth in the world. Moreover, a sound system of normal universities, schools, and teachers' training courses will be set up to train competent teachers.

Section 10
Science and Technology

1. The strategy of setting up a system of technology complex will be carried out

To realize industrialization and to meet the challenge of the new technological revolution are two unified, strategic tasks required for the development of our science and technology towards 2000. Thus, it is of paramount importance for us to handle correctly the relationship between high technologies and traditional technologies. In this connection, we must treat traditional and high technologies as an organic whole, developing both simultaneously. The development of high technologies must be incorporated into the transformation of traditional technologies and industries, so that the whole system of traditional technologies will embody the characteristics of high technologies. Therefore, what is developed will be a technology complex in which traditional technologies and high technologies are closely linked with each other, rather than a system of traditional technologies in its original meaning. Based on this strategy of development, by the end of this century high technologies and traditional technologies will be fused to form a number of mixed technologies. Thus, our task of industrialization could be accomplished on the basis of a relatively high level of technology. Beginning from the early years of the twenty-first century, our priorities will be gradually shifted to the development of high technologies, and our economy is expected to expanded rapidly thereafter.

2. The value of knowledge in society will enhance enormously

As the reform of the economic structure and the system of science and technology goes deeper, our economy will have a strong inherent demand for science and technology. By the end of this century, the technology market will become an important component part of our market system, and a new scientific and technological system inseparable from society and economy will be gradually formed. A fundamental change in the value of knowledge will take place. The extremely important role of knowledge in the creation of wealth will be recognized by society. Consequently, scientific and technological personnel as carriers of knowledge will be greatly respected by the whole society, and their role will be brought into full play. Moreover, by the year 2000, those working on the scientific and technological fronts will mainly be young people.

3. The task of China's industrialization will be basically accomplished

By the end of this century, our traditional technologies and industries will tend to mature. High technologies and newly emerging industries will become important factors in the development of our national economy. It is expected that China will have a much solid technological foundation and a much higher technological level than what the West had during its initial period of industrialization.

4. Our scientific and technological level will be raised markedly

By the year 2000, China will have a contingent of scientists of international caliber in the fields of basic and applied research work. In some fields, such as mathematics, astronomy, life science, and geoscience, we will probably hold leading positions in the world. In some fields of engineering sciences, such as information, material science, microelectronics, photoelectronics, theory of electromagnetic field, and mechanical sciences, notable developments can be expected. In some frontier technologies, such as super-high tension, cryogenics, superconductivity, and superpurity, some breakthroughs will probably be made.

It is expected that China's comprehensive technologies will reach the level of the developed countries at the end of the 1970s and early 1980s by the year 2000. In some fields such as the petroleum industry, the petrochemical industry, mechanical technologies, and microelectronics technologies, we are likely to reach the levels of the developed countries of the 1990s in some aspects.

The progress in our science and technology will enhance our country's competitive capabilities. Technology-intensive products, such as machinery and electrical products, chemical products, new materials, optical fiber, laser machines, as well as color TV sets and electronic sewing machines, will form a significant proportion of our industrial output value. Some of our quality products, such a light industrial products, textiles, handicrafts, mineral products, and foodstuffs will be more competitive in the world market.

5. Science and technology will be developed vigorously in rural areas

China's rural areas will witness notable changes by the end of this century. Without moving to the urban areas, several hundred million farmers will change their occupations from farming to other trades. Science and technology will be the most active and dynamic factors behind these earth-shaking changes. Meanwhile, several million township enterprises will come into existence in the rural areas. They will not only engage in traditional industrial production such as the processing of agricultural and sideline products, construction, foodstuffs, transportation, and mining, but also high-tech and newly-emerging industries such as the bioengineering and microelectronics sectors. Both agriculture and industry will be developed vigorously in the rural areas. The differences between town and country will be reduced.

6. The open policy will be further implemented in science and

technology

There will be more frequent contacts between the scientific and technological circles of our country and their counterparts in other countries. The contacts will take a variety of forms, and cooperation will develop in depth and scope. China will send more scholars, specialists, and students to work or study in other countries and international science and technology organizations. Meanwhile, more and more scientific and technological workers from various countries will come to China to work in our research institutions or even factories and enterprises. More joint research work will be conducted by various types of our research institutions with those of other countries. China will participate in a series of international projects of scientific and technological cooperation involving broad areas of science and technology including "soft" sciences. China will become an active force in international scientific and technological activities. The gap between China and the developed countries in science and technology will be narrowed by the end of this century.

CHAPTER III
A RELATIVELY COMFORTA-
BLE STANDARD OF LIVING
FOR THE CHINESE PEOPLE

Section 1
Basic Concepts of Consumption and a Relatively Comfortable Standard of Living

1. The concept of consumption

The concept of consumption has a broad sense as well as a narrow sense. In its narrow sense, it refers to consumption in people's daily lives, while in its broad sense, it also includes consumption of materials and manpower in the course of production. In our discussion here, we refer to consumption in its narrow sense.

As links in the economic movement, consumption and production act upon each other. The purpose of socialist production is to constantly satisfy the people's increasing needs in material and cultural life. However, under the influence of "left" ideas, this problem was not given due attention over a long period in the past. In our study of this question, we are trying to cast off the old model and adopt a new approach. Starting from a population forecast and ending at the realization of a fairly comfortable life for the people, we incorporated economic, cultural, scientific, technological, and social demands in our study.

People's diversified needs given rise to the substance and pattern of consumption. Studying consumption patterns promotes coordination between consumption demand and the production of consumer goods, not only coordination in the total amount but also in the pattern. Thus, the study of the level and pattern of consumption is of great importance for China's modernization drive as well as for the realization of a fairly comfortable life for the people by the end of this century.

Consumption level refers to the total amount consumed by the consumers in a given period. Expressed in terms of money of the currency year, it is called the nominal consumption level. Taking a certain period as basis and after adjusting for price rises, it is called actual consumption level. All the data quoted in this book are actual consumption levels calculated in terms of the constant prices of 1980. As there are numerous kinds and types of consumer goods with vast differences in quality, and all these constantly change, it is extremely difficult, almost impossible, to measure consumption levels in kind.

Classification according to the type of consumers, consumption can be categorized into personal consumption and social consumption. Personal consumption demand, or effective consumption demand, is invariably restricted by income and affected by the prices of consumer goods. Welfare items enjoyed by individuals are included in social consumption in our study.

The substance of consumption includes not only material consumer goods but should also include consumptive labor. Hence, the analysis and study of the laws governing labor consumption are indispensable.

Consumption pattern refers to the classification of certain consumer goods and labor. The classification can be made from different angles. Using the methods of classification of Adam Smith, Engels divided consumer goods into three categories: those for subsistence, those for enjoyment, and those for development. This method of classification is of great theoretical significance as it epitomizes the trend of development of consumption demand. However, as the standards of this kind of classification are not very clear, it is very difficult to put some consumer goods under the right category when making a quantitative analysis. Consequently, most people divide consumer goods according to their functions, such as food, clothing, and articles for daily use.

The classification is based on the purpose of study and the data available, ranging from three to four to over 100 categories. Most Chinese and foreign economists confine the number of categories to ten or so for the convenience of study. To make a comprehensive quantitative study of the consumption patterns, it is necessary to divide consumption patterns into various categories. In the study and forecasts of "China Towards the Year 2000," various methods of classification are used, including forecasts of consumption levels and consumption patterns by means of mathematical models. This book has quoted various schemes and results to facilitate our analysis.

2. The concept of a fairly comfortable standard of living

Engel's law sums up the changes in the pattern of personal consumption. It can be briefly put this way: With an increase in income, the amount spent on food as a proportion of total expenditures gradually declines. Thus, the proportion of food consumption compared to total consumption (called the Engel coefficient of food expenditure) can be taken as an indication of the standard of living. The United Nations Food and Agriculture Organization has roughly defined that when the Engel coefficient is between 50-59 percent, it represents a life with adequate food and clothing; when it is between 40-50 percent, it represents a well-off life; when it is between 20-40 percent, it represents an affluent life.

The Engel coefficient presupposes that the monetary expenditure of an individual household covers all of its consumption. However, the monetary expenditure of the Chinese people cannot reflect all their actual consumption. For instance, some of the people's consumption such as urban housing, medical services, education, and some social services comes under the category of welfare subsidy. It is estimated that the welfare benefit enjoyed by each urban worker or staff member, such as public medical services, children's education, social insurance, and housing rent subsidy, amounts to 6 percent of his or her annual wage. Thus, a large share of the monetary expenditure in personal consumption is for food, clothing, and articles of daily use, particularly on food. In such circumstances, calculations made according to the Engel coefficient have to take social consumption into consideration.

The target of achieving a fairly comfortable standard of living by the end of this century was set forth in the light of China's national conditions. It has to reach the general international standard and has to be in keeping with the level of China's economic development. Compared with the developed countries, our present average per-capita consumption level is very low. However, as there is even distribution of income, the prices of basic necessities of daily life are relatively stable, and the people enjoy many kinds of welfare benefits from the state, the gap with developed countries is not as big as it may seem.

Our well-off standard of living should find expression in the substance of consumption and the quality of life. The quality of life is affected by expenditures on personal consumption as well as by such factors as social consumption, ecological environment, and cultural life. When the consumption level is fixed by and large, we should effectively improve the quality of people's lives so that the substance of life will reflect modern material civilization and the results of modern science and technology and embody the demand for a socialist civilization with advanced culture and technology. In short, it should be imbued with the flavor of our time and help people's overall development. These are the characteristics of a fairly well-off standard of living for our country.

Section 2
Consumption Levels and Consumption Patterns

1. The people's rising standard of living

The people's consumption level has something to do with national strength. After making a forecast of the general economic strength and level of development, we have to fix the proportion of distribution between accumulation and consumption in national income. While fixing the accumulation rate, we have to avoid committing the error of high accumulation and low consumption and have to fix an appropriate consumption rate so that it will not grow too fast to the detriment of the country's development. Our basic principle is to improve the people's standard of living step by step on the basis of steady, sustained, and coordinated growth of the national economy.

By the end of this century, the Chinese people's consumption level will reach 712.3 yuan (calculated in terms of the constant prices of 1980), 3.14 times that of 1980, as shown in Table 3-1.

Table 3-1
PEOPLE'S CONSUMPTION LEVELS AT THE END OF THIS CENTURY
(calculated in terms of the constant prices of 1980)

	2000	Increase over 1980 (percent)	Average rate of 1980–2000 (percent)
Gross national product (GNP) (billion yuan)	1,977	340	7.7
Average per-capita GNP (yuan)	1,584.4	250	6.4
National income (billion yuan)	1,449.89	290	7.1
Average per-capita national income (yuan)	1,161.8	210	5.9
Social consumption (billion yuan)	123.29	310	7.4
Personal consumption (billion yuan)	888.94	300	7.2
Personal consumption level (yuan)	712.3	210	5.9
Total amount of consumer goods supply (billion yuan)	709.83 (scheme 1) 840 (scheme 2)	310*	7.7** 8.0

* Increase over 1981.
** The average increase of 1981-2000.

After over 30 years of national reconstruction, China has turned from a backward agricultural state into a strong socialist country with a complete range of industries. From 1952 to 1982, national income increased from 58.9 billion yuan to 424.7 billion yuan. after adjusting for price rises, it registered a 5.8-fold increase. But in the same period, the population increased from 574.82 million to 1,015.41 million, and the rise of national income came mainly from the building of new enterprises. Consequently, the average per-capita national income increased only by 3.3 fold. Owing to the lack of efficiency and the influence of the "left" line, high accumulation failed to push ahead the country's development as it should and instead curbed the people's consumption. Between 1952 and 1980, the people's average per-capita consumption level rose by 2.6 percent annually, while between 1980 and 2000, the average annual growth will be 5.9 percent. The rate of improvement of people's standard of living in these two decades will be 2.27 times that of the 28 years from 1952 to 1980.

In 1980, the consumption level of the people throughout the country was 227 yuan, that of urban residents was 468 yuan, and that of rural residents 173 yuan. The ratio between urban and rural areas was 2.7:1. By 2000, the consumption level of the people throughout the country will reach 712 yuan, that of urban residents will be 1,209 yuan, and that of rural residents 650 yuan. the ratio between urban and rural areas will be 1.86:1. the difference in the standard of living between urban and rural people will be gradually narrowed. It is a general trend that with the growth of our economy, the gap between the consumption levels of urban and rural people will gradually shrink. In studying this question, we should take note of the fact that there is a considerably high rate of self-sufficiency in the production of China's rural people. Before 1981, the rate was above 50 percent, which dropped to 44 percent in 1981. With the rise in the percentage of marketable products in the rural areas, the rate of self-sufficiency will further reduce. However, the rural people's expenditures are not so extensive as that of the urban people who spend more on transport, services, and cultural and recreational actiyities. It is estimated that when the ratio between the consumption levels for the urban and rural people reaches 1.5:1, the actual standard of living of rural people will be close to that of urban residents. Judging from the principle of distribution according to work, the average national income created by urban residents is higher than that of rural residents, and thus the difference between town and country will not be reduced too fast in a short period of time.

Between 1952 and 1980, the national income increased by an average of 6 percent annually while the people's standard of living rose 2.6 percent. The ratio between the two being 2.31:1. The policy of high accumulation practiced in the past displayed insufficient regard for the people's increasing demands for material and cultural life. One-sided emphasis on the development of production overlooked the building of supporting infrastructure facilities, resulting in a disproportionate industrial structure and caused pressure from two sides: the stepping up of the building of infrastructure facilities while readjusting the industrial structure and the rapid raising of the people's standard of living while developing production. Between 1980 and 1985, national income increased by an average of 8.2 percent annually, while the people's average per-capita income rose by 7.1 percent, the ratio between the two being 1.15:1. This is an indication that much remained to be done in improving the people's standard of living in the past and that great efforts have been made in this respect in the past few years. Between 1980 and 2000, national income will increase by annual rate of 7.1 percent, while the people's average per-capita income will rise 5.9 percent annually. The ratio between the two will be 1.2:1, lower than the 2.31:1 in the past but higher than the 1.15:1 registered between 1980 and 1985. This shows we will enter a period of stable, coordinated development of production and the people's standard of living.

2. An analysis of the changes in the people's consumption patterns

Food accounts for half of the Chinese people's consumption today. The proportion of urban residents' expenditures on food to their total expenditures dropped from 68 percent in 1952 to 56.66 percent in 1981. It will be further reduced to 48 percent, 46 percent, 44 percent, or 40 percent (according to different schemes envisaged) by 2000. According to the provisions of the Engel coefficient, this will be a comparatively comfortable standard of living for the Chinese people.

Chinese and foreign nutritionists believe that the average quantity of heat absorbed by the Chinese people has reached the required level, though the intake of protein and fat is much lower than that of the developed countries. China should choose the food pattern suited to our country's conditions and the demand for modernization. The food pattern will undergo certain changes. The proportion of staple foods will drop by certain extent while that of meat, dairy products, eggs, vegetables, and fruits may go up. But we should not seek high animal protein and fat. With the development of the food industry and the full utilization of all kinds of resources, food processing will steadily increase in scope and depth, and all kinds of instant foods, semi-finished products, and finished products will be available to consumers.

The amount spent on clothing as a portion of total consumption will rise from 16.8 percent in 1981 to 19.5 percent in 1990s. By 2000, the absolute amount of expenditures on clothing will increase steadily, but its proportion to total expenditures will not change very much. This demonstrates that with a rising standard of living, people no longer seek garments that are long-lasting but prefer comfortable, beautiful, tasteful clothes that reflect age, professional status, and are adaptable to weather changes. Under the spur of such desires for consumption, expenditures on clothing will increase swiftly in the days to come. However, after a certain period, the demand for durable consumer goods and the pursuit of cultural life will gain the upper hand.

In the midst of this trend of increased consumption, expenditures on durable consumer goods will continue to go up between now and the end of the century both in its absolute amount and in its share of the total expenditures. The increase in expenditures on durable consumer goods reflects the consumer psychology that after the demand for basic daily necessities are met, people hope to enjoy a more comfortable and easier life. Correspondingly, the demand for electric power will steadily increase.

The proportion of expenditures on labor service or non-commodity expenditures for both urban and rural residents will go up. This not only will ease the pressure on material consumption but will meet the people's growing needs and conform to the world trend of consumption. Aside from the increase in water and electricity charges arising from increases in the number of domestic electrical appliances, the people's expenses will mainly involve costs for travel fares, tourism, service charges for daily life, and recreational activities.

The expenditure on housing will rise steadily as the floor space of living quarters of both urban and rural residents will increase sizably.

3. Forecasts of the consumption levels and consumption patterns of different areas

China is a multinational country with a vast territory. Owing to natural conditions and historical reasons, the economic development of different areas is highly unbalanced. This effects consumption levels and patterns. The authors of the report "Chinese People's Consumption Towards the Year 2000" considered this problem. The report divides China into three areas: the coastal developed area, the central plains area, and the outlying area. The consumption level and consumption pattern of the outlying area were calculated on the basis of materials gathered from Guizhou and Gansu provinces and the Ningxia Hui Autonomous Region. With regional subsidies, the wages of workers and staff in this area are higher than those of the coastal and central plains areas, while the income of peasants in this area is much lower than those of the two other areas. To reflect such differences, we confined our forecasts to the consumption levels and patterns of the rural areas only.

Table 3-2

CONSUMPTION LEVEL AND PATTERN OF
THE COASTAL DEVELOPED AREA

	Average for urban and rural residents		Rural residents
Average per-capita annual expenditure on consumption (yuan)	Minimum 950	Maximum 1200	700
Consumption structure (percent)			
Food	45	43	46
Clothing	11.5	11	11
Articles for daily use	15.5	17	13
Fuel	3	2.5	3
Housing	17.5	18.5	21
Non-commodity expenditures	7.5	8	6

Table 3-3

CONSUMPTION LEVEL AND PATTERN OF
THE CENTRAL PLAIN AREA

	Average for urban and rural residents	Rural residents
Average per-capita annual expenditure on consumption (yuan)	630	560
Consumption structure (percent)		
Food	48	49
Clothing	13	12
Articles for daily use	17	15
Fuel	2.4	3
Housing	14	17
Non-commodity expenditures	5.6	4

Table 3-4

CONSUMPTION LEVEL AND PATTERN OF
THE OUTLYING AREA

	Low limit	Middle limit	High limit
Average per-capita annual expenditure on consumption (yuan)	318	374	475
Consumption structure (percent)			
Food	56	54	52
Clothing	14	13.5	13
Articles for daily use	11.5	12.5	13.3
Fuel	5	4.5	4.2
Housing	10	12	13.5
Non-commodity expenditures	3.5	3.2	4

In addition, the trend of changes in the consumption level of the rural residents of Jiangsu and Gansu provinces was also analyzed. By 2000, the average per-capita consumption expenditure of rural residents in Gansu will be 374 yuan, amounting to 37 percent of the 1,017 yuan in Jiangsu. This shows that the consumption level of the rural residents in Gansu is 15 years behind that of Jiangsu. This possible trend warrants attention.

4. The effect of financial subsidies on the consumption levels of urban residents

Thanks to subsidies for grain, cotton, oil, eggs, and other items, there is a big gap between the actual and nominal standard of living of urban residents. If, with the price reform, subsidies for grain, oil, non-staple foods, coal, cotton, wadding, rent, traffic, and heating were abolished, while subsidies for collective social welfare, enterprises welfare, visiting close relatives, labor protection, and medical services were retained, the impact would be tremendous. As a result of the subsidies, each person in the non-

non-agricultural population of the cities received an annual benefit of 286 yuan in 1982. Suppose each worker or staff member undertook the family burden of 1.73 persons, then he or she received a benefit of 494.78 yuan, amounting to 62 percent of the average annual wage of 798 yuan. If this is added to the wage of each worker or staff member, then his or her annual wage would come to 1,293 yuan.

The total amount of various kinds of price subsidies in 1982 made up about 74 percent of the total financial subsidies. Among the state price subsidies, more than 75 percent were for grain, oil, meat, eggs, poultry, and cotton. As a result of the irrational price system, the more output for these products, the greater the financial burden will be for the state. It would be a recommendable policy measure for the state to abolish some of the financial subsidies and make rational arrangement for economic development and the people's lives in conjunction with the reform of the price and wage system.

Section 3
Forecasts of Consumer Goods Production

1. The general level of development of consumer goods

It is predicted that by 2000 the gross output value of consumer goods will reach about 1,110 billion yuan, 4.2 times that of 1980. With improvement of the people's diet, the food industry will develop enormously. There are two forecast schemes about the output value of the food industry by 2000: one envisions a 4.5-fold increase over that of 1980, the other a 5-fold increase. Industrial food products consumed by urban and rural residents will account for around 50 percent of their total expenditures on food. With the rise in the amount of clothing required, the pattern of textile production will change. The rate of ready-made clothes will rise from 20 percent in the 1980s to 50 percent and above. The quantity, quality, specifications, and varieties of textiles and garments will basically meet the people's needs and provide some for export. By the end of this century, the output value of the textile industry will be 3.8 times that of 1980.

There are also two forecast schemes for the total volume of retail sales of consumer goods by the end of this century: one is 710 billion yuan and the other 840 billion yuan, both being calculated in terms of the constant prices of 1980.

China's consumer goods production not only will meet the needs of the people's daily lives but will also turn out new products that are competitive in the international market. To meet the people's rising standard of living, efforts should be made to develop products in short supply which can help withdraw currency from circulation. The differences in consumption levels among the Chinese people will gradually widen. The needs of different levels of consumption should be taken into consideration hereafter. We should explore the possibility of a greater number of motor cars being owned by individuals and families and the tremendous changes in the people's consumption patterns which will come with the introduction of the program of commercialized housing. We should not only cater to the needs of the domestic market but should sell our consumer goods on the international market in exchange for imports.

2. The development of the agro-food industry will be accelerated

The development of the food industry hinges on agricultural production and the rate of marketable agricultural products. Grain and oil-bearing crops are the basic raw materials for the food industry, and they have a vital bearing on the basic needs of people's material lives. It is estimated that the total output of grain crops will reach 500 million tons by 2000, with an average per-capita share of 400 kilograms.

By 2000, China's sugar output will be 12 million tons, achieving the target of quadrupling the output and doubling the area planted to sugarcane and beet root. The average per-capita annual consumption of sugar will reach 10 kilograms, 100 percent higher than the present level.

Initial forecasts show that compared with 1980, the output of sterilized milk, dairy products, and egg products will increase by more than 20 times by 2000; food for babies, children, and old people and beer and beverage will increase by more than 15 times; bean products, bread, and other flour-made products and fruit and vegetable products will increase by more than 10 times.

3. In the development of textiles, we should pay equal attention to cotton cloth and chemical fiber cloth, with the stress laid on supplying ready-made clothes

To match the people's rising purchasing power, China's per-capita consumption of chemical fibers should increase to 5.6 kilograms on average by 2000 (the world average is expected to reach 8-8.5 kilograms) from 3.2 kilograms in 1980 (the world average was 6.7 kilograms). Natural fiber will continue to play a dominant role in our textile industry in this century. The pattern of textile production will go through a major readjustment, and the areas of their use will be steadily widened. The proportion of textiles used for garments, decoration, and production will be readjusted from 80:7:13 in 1980 to 60:20:20 in 2000 (the present ratio in developed countries is roughly 40:30:30).

4. Durable consumer goods and new consumer goods will be developed rapidly and constantly updated

It is predicted that compared with 1980, the supply of TV sets will increase by about 26 times, refrigerators by about 160 times, and washing machines by about 60 times. The market demand for bicycles, sewing machines, watches, and radios has become stable. In the late 1980s, the sales of such products in the cities reached the saturation point, and some have shown a declining trend. There is still a market in the rural areas, but the growth in sales will also slow down there. Production of such commodities has to be planned according to market demand in order to avoid overstocking and waste.

On the basis of meeting the basic needs for subsistence, it is necessary to steadily increase production of new consumer goods. It is estimated that in the late 1980s and 1990s, electrical products (such as video recorders), information products (such as computers for management of small enterprises and for family education), health and fitness products (such as miniature passenger and freight trucks used by peasants), agricultural products processing machinery, and new materials for interior and exterior decoration will develop considerably.

5. Two forecasts have been made on housing conditions in the urban areas (including industrial and mining areas)

One forecast is that the average per-capita living space of urban residents will increase from 4.6 square meters in 1983 to 8 square meters in 2000; and the other put the figure at 10 square meters. We believe that the former forecast conforms more to reality. By the end of the century, each family will live in a fairly comfortable apartment with an average of 8 square meters of living space for each person. This will be roughly equal to the level of Japan in the 1960s, of the Eastern European countries in the 1970s, and of the Soviet Union in the early 1980s.

The average of 8 square meters of living space per person amounts to 12 square meters of usable floor space. Considering the differences caused by various factors, the average per-capita living space of some families will exceed 8 square meters, while other families will be below this figure.

The targets of housing for rural areas (including rural towns) indicate that average per-capita housing will increase from about 11 square meters in 1983 to more than 15 square meters by 2000; that of each person will have a room to live in; and that the quality of housing will improve considerably.

6. Housing construction will continue to develop to meet the needs of rising living conditions

By the end of 1983, a total of 1.265 billion square meters of urban housing had been completed. It is predicted that by 2000, 945 million square meters of these houses will be retained for use. In addition, 2.55-2.8 billion square meters of new housing will be constructed in the 17 years between 1984 and 2000.

Section 4

The Picture of a Relatively Comfortable Standard of Living

1. Average per-capita GNP will reach about 1,000 U.S. dollars

When the Chinese people achieve a relatively comfortable standard of living by the end of this century, the average per-capita GNP of the Chinese people will reach about 1,000 U.S. dollars. The average consumption level of all families in the country will be higher than the level of middle-income families in cities at present. The average per-capita annual consumption level of urban and rural residents in the country will be 712 yuan in terms of 1980 prices, or 3.1 times the 227 yuan in 1980. The people's basic needs will be met, and they will have some money to spare. As China's consumption patterns and price system are different from those of the Western countries, compared with foreign currencies, the purchasing power of the Chinese currency (renminbi) for basic means of subsistence is much higher than the official exchange rate. Thus, the difference between the Chinese purchasing power and that of foreign countries is smaller than what the currency may indicate. Using the prices of 74 consumer goods and labor services as the bases for calculation, Chinese and foreign experts forecast that the actual level of the well- off life to be attained by the Chinese people at the end of this century will amount to a living standard based on an annual income of 1,400 U.S. dollars in the United States.

2. The difference in the consumption levels between China's urban and rural areas will narrow

By the turn of this century, the difference between urban and rural consumption levels will narrow from 2.7:1 in 1980 to 1.8:1. However, the differences between regions and among the peasants and workers and staff will tend to enlarge. Hence, the comparatively well-off life to be attained will inevitably have different levels. Some people will outstrip the well-off level and enjoy a life of affluence, and some will just be adequately fed and clothed.

3. Consumption patterns will continue in an upward trend

Consumption patterns will continue upward with the trend of modernization and will reach the level of a well-off standard of living. The most striking feature is that the proportion spent on food of the total consumption expenditures will be 40-45 percent, thus meeting the international definition that this percentage should be lower than 50 percent in order for a well-off standard of living to be achieved.

4. The character of consumption will change

The means of subsistence will continue to be the principal part of consumption, the means of development will have an important place in consumption, and the means of enjoyment will make up a certain proportion of total expenditures. With the material life basically satisfied, cultural life will become an important aspect of consumption. As redoubled efforts will be made to build a socialist society with advanced culture and ideology, the quality of the people will improve markedly.

Junior high school education will become universal in the rural areas. Senior high school or vocational education will become basically universal in big and medium-sized cities. The rate of enrollment of university students will increase from the present 5 percent to about 15 percent. The number of illiterates and semi-illiterates will drop from 23.6 percent in the 1980s to about 5 percent. By then, all illiterates will be above 55 years of age.

5. Consumption will be further diversified and socialized

Material and cultural life will be richer and more colorful. Labor service consumption will increase. By the end of this century, our urban and rural residents' expenditures on labor consumption as a portion of their total consumption expenditures will increase to 10 percent. By then, the residents' living conditions and social services will be greatly improved. Telephones will be installed in middle-income families, and public telephones will become universal. Domestic tourism will be in vogue but will still be restricted by payment ability, conditions of transport, and tourist facilities. The time spent on household work will be reduced considerably. Working hours will be shortened adequately so that people will have more time for study, social contact, recreational activities, and all-round development.

6. The Chinese people's food patterns will have Chinese characteristics and modern features

Both the nutritional value and quality of food will improved substantially. There will be fresh vegetables, vegetable protein products, and a certain amount of meat and eggs at the family dining table every day. Most of the children will be well fed. There will be a rich variety of processed food. Urban families will be supplied with large quantities of instant food, but most families will choose to cook their meals.

7. People's taste in clothing will change

Urban residents will prefer clothes which are comfortable, beautiful, varied, and reflect individuality and the fashions of the times. However, people of different age groups and professions have vastly different demands for clothing and its updating. The amount spent on clothing will steadily increase, but in the 1990s, clothing expenses as a proportion of total expenditures will tend to become stable. The rural residents' clothing will improve greatly in quality, quantity, and variety. But generally speaking, there will be clear differences in clothing between urban and rural people.

8. Domestic electric appliances will become popular

Electric appliances such as TV sets, refrigerators and washing machines will become popular in urban families in general and in the families of rural areas with an income above the middle level. A considerable number of families will have video recorders, computers for family education, and electronic pianos. But air conditioners, which consume a lot of electricity, will be restricted. The quality of furniture will rise steadily. By the end of this century, we will not only have the household electronic products which have been popular in economically developed countries, but we will also have domestic-made electronic products which conform to our national conditions. The use of domestic electrical appliances will be restricted not only by the people's ability to pay but also by the supply of electricity.

Bicycles will remain the major means of transportation along with buses. Only a small number of families will have motor cars or miniature passenger and freight trucks.

9. Housing conditions will improve immensely

The average per-capita housing floor space for urban residents will reach more than 8 square meters (usable floor space will reach 12 square meters). Basically each family will have an apartment. In the rural areas, each person will have 15 square meters of housing. The structure of the houses will improve, and infrastructure facilities, such as water supply and drainage and roads, will be in much better condition. The commercialization of housing will be universally introduced in cities, and some urban residents will own their own houses.

10. Public welfare funding will be reformed

Public welfare undertakings will be paid for with public funds instead of being financed entirely by the government. This will accelerate their development. The medical conditions for urban and rural residents will improve. Life expectancy will increase from 68 years in the 1980s to 72 years and above at the end of this century, a range comparable to that of developed countries.

"China's Economy Towards the Year 2000," "The Chinese People's Consumption Towards the Year 2000," "Overall Quantitative Analysis of China's Economy Towards the Year 2000," as well as the general report "China Towards the Year 2000" have all studied the question of the Chinese people's standard of living at the end of this century. The results of these studies have provided reference materials in writing this chapter.

CHAPTER IV
CHINA'S ECONOMIC STRUCTURE

Section 1
Retrospect of Structural Changes in China

1. Transformation of the major sectors of the economy

In 1949, China was mainly an agricultural country. Its total output value of industry and agriculture was 46.6 billion yuan, of which the total output value of agriculture was 32.6 billion yuan and that of industry was 14 billion yuan. Changes in major economic activities from 1952 to 1985 are shown in Tables 4-1 and 4-2.

Table 4-1

STRUCTURAL CHANGES OF THE ECONOMY
(Based upon the price of current year)

(%)

	1952	1957	1970	1980	1985
Primary sector	52.1	42.2	37.0	34.5	35.9
Secondary sector	21.7	30.7	40.4	46.5	42.3
Tertiary sector	26.2	27.1	22.6	19.0	21.8

Table 4-2

STRUCTURAL CHANGES OF THE LABOR FORCE

(%)

	1952	1957	1970	1980	1985
Primary sector	83.5	81.2	80.8	72.1	62.5
Secondary sector	7.4	9.0	10.2	16.3	21.1
Tertiary sector	9.1	9.8	9.0	11.6	16.4

Due to the differences in the methods of calculation of the national economy and the disrupting influence of the "cultural revolution" (1966-76) on statistical work, the figures in Table 4-1 and Table 4-2 can be taken only as as a reference.

2. Structural Changes of Industries

The transformation of the industrial structure is shown in Table 4-3. It should also be pointed out that the classification of Chinese industrial branches is different from that of the international standard. The numbers in Table 4-3 show the percentage of the output value of each sector in relation to the gross industrial output value. The bracketed number shows the rank of the percentage share. Figures in Table 4-3 give the trends

Table 4-3

STRUCTURAL CHANGES OF INDUSTRIES

Branch	1952	1957	1975	1981
Metallurgical industry	5.9 (5)	9.3 (3)	9.0 (5)	8.0 (5)
Electric power industry	1.3 (10)	1.4 (8)	3.9 (7)	3.7 (7)
Coal mining industry	2.4 (8)	2.3 (7)	2.8 (9)	2.2 (9)
Petroleum industry	0.5 (11)	0.9 (9)	5.6 (6)	4.7 (6)
Chemical engineering industry	4.8 (6)	8.2 (4)	11.3 (4)	12.5 (3)
Machine building industry	11.4 (3)	18.2 (2)	27.7 (1)	23.6 (1)
Construction material industry	3.0 (7)	3.3 (6)	3.1 (8)	3.5 (8)
Lumbering industry	6.5 (4)	5.4 (5)	1.9 (10)	1.7 (10)
Food industry	24.1 (2)	19.6 (1)	12.0 (3)	12.3 (4)
Textile industry	27.5 (1)	18.2 (2)	12.3 (2)	16.7 (2)
Paper making industry	2.2 (9)	2.3 (7)	1.3 (11)	1.2 (11)

of structural changes in the past which is helpful in judging the future direction of the change.

We can see from Table 4-3 that the changes of rank in terms of percentage shares of the 11 industrial branches from 1952 to 1981 are as follows:

(a) Industries whose percentages rose steadily: Machine-building, petroleum, power, and chemical industries;

(b) Industries whose percentages went down significantly: Papermaking, lumbering, and food industries;

(c) Industries whose percentages went down slightly: Textile, coal, and building materials industries;

(d) Industry whose percentages remained basically unchanged: Metallurgical industry.

As the figures cited in Table 4-3 are based on the price system, the distortion of the price system may not provide a true picture, so the growth rate of certain major products of these industries is given in Table 4-4 for cross check.

The serial number in Table 4-4 corresponds with the industrial branch listed in Table 4-3. The products selected may not be representative to show the order of importance of the respective industry. But if we assume that the average growth rate of the products of that industry can represent the growth rate of the industry roughly, the order in terms of growth rate for these industries would be as follows: Petroleum industry — machine-building industry — power industry — metallurgical industry — building materials industry — papermaking industry — coal mining industry — textile industry — food industry — lumbering industry.

3. Development of the tertiary industry

In the past, China did not have an exact definition for tertiary industry. As a result, many problems had been encountered due to the neglect of the development of this sector. According to SIC standard, the tertiary sector is classified in the following:

Transport, communications and utilities;

Wholesale and retail trade;

Finance, insurance, and real estate;

Table 4-4

GROWTH OF MAJOR INDUSTRIAL PRODUCTS OF
DIFFERENT INDUSTRIES

Product	1952	1980	Average growth rate (%)
Pig iron (million tons)	1.93	38.02	11.2
Steel (million tons)	1.35	37.12	12.5
Electricity (billion kwh)	7.3	300.6	14.2
Crude coal (million tons)	66	620	8.3
Crude oil (million tons)	0.44	105.95	21.6
Chemical fertilizer (thousand tons)	39	12,320	22.8
Caustic soda (thousand tons)	79	1,923	12
Plastics (thousand tons)	2	898	24.3
Power generating equipment (MW)	6	4,193	26.3
Mining equipment (thousand tons)	1.8	163	17.4
Machine tools (thousand units)	13.7	134.0	8.4
Internal combustion engines (thousand hp)	40	25,390	25.9
Cement (million tons)	2.86	79.86	12.6
Plate glass (million std cases)	2.13	27.71	9.5
Timber (million cu. meters)	11.20	53.59	5.7
Sugar (thousand tons)	451	2,570	6.4
Salt (thousand tons)	4,945	17,280	4.5
Tobacco (thousand cases)	265	1,520	6.4
Wine (thousand tons)	23	368.5	10.4
Cotton yarn (thousand tons)	656	2,930	5.4
Cotton cloth (billion M)	3.83	13.47	4.6
Woolen piece goods (million M)	4.23	101	11.9
Machine made paper and paper board	372	5,350	9.98

Services (including personnel and business services);
Government.

The following is a further discussion about some of those
mentioned above.

(a) Transport

The growth of the transport sector is not properly matched with other industrial activities, which can be shown from the relatively low average growth of this sector.

Table 4-5

SOME INDICATORS OF THE TRANSPORT SECTOR

Item	1952	1980	Average growth rate (%)
Freight traffic volume (billion tons/km)	73.4	849.6	9.1
Passenger traffic volume (billion passengers/km)	24.9	228.1	8.2

(b) Communications and postal service

The communications and postal service has also not properly developed in comparison with other economic activities. For instance, in 1980 the number of telephone sets for per 100 people in the world was 10, while that of China and India was 0.4 only. China and the United States are nearly of the same territorial size, but the United States had 1.8 million long-distance communications channels, which is 16 times that of India and 75 times that of China.

(c) Due to the neglect of the development of commodity exchange, the average growth rate of the commercial sector is also slower than other economic sectors. The average growth rate of the total volume of retail sales was 11.37 percent in the First Five-Year Plan period. It was lowered to 6.77 percent from the Second Five-Year Plan period to the the Fifth Five-Year Plan period. In the First Five-Year Plan period, the number of the retail organizations had been reduced around 50 percent in comparison with the figure of 1952, and people employed in this sector was reduced by 20 percent. The average number of people engaged in commercial services for per 10,000 people was 117.8. The figure was further lowered to 63 in 1978. The situation was corrected after 1978, with the figure rising to 242 in 1985.

(d) Other services

The financial system plays an important role in changing the system of direct control over economic activities to one of indirect control and serving to mobilize more savings deposits for investment for further industrialization. Although China's financial system has undergone major changes in the past, but its role, compared to the financial systems of other developing countries, is still quite limited. There is great room for further development and improvement for both banking and non-banking institutions.

Section 2
Changes and Prospects for Consumption Patterns

1. Prospects for future structural change

Prospects of structural changes in China towards the year 2000 will be projected and analyzed from various aspects so that a proper conclusion can be derived. In fact, however, the conclusion of this book is derived from both qualitative and quantitative analysis, through the international comparative studies, through the analysis of supply constraints and factors of production, and through the collection of opinions of various experts and institutions.

2. Forecast of consumption patterns

Many complex factors are involved in the forecast of consumption patterns, which is made more difficult under the conditions of price readjustment and reform of the economic structure.

Consumption patterns are related to the classification of certain consumer goods and labor services, which can be conducted from different angles. One kind of classification is to divide the consumer goods into three categories: means of subsistence, means of enjoyment, and means of development. This kind of classification can summarize the trend of development of consumption needs, but it can only be used to make some qualitative analysis because the method of classification are not very clear, and it is hard to determine in which category some of the consumer goods should belong. Experts believe that by the end of this century the means of subsistence will remain the principal part of the Chinese people's consumption, the means of development will have an important place, and the means of enjoyment will make up a certain proportion. Consumption will be further diversified and socialized. Household labor will be lessened. The people will have more time for study, recreation, and rest, and their material and cultural lives will become richer and more colorful.

To make a quantitative analysis, we use two methods of classification to show consumption patterns. One method is to classify consumer goods according to their functions such as food, clothing, and articles for daily use. The other method is to classify consumer goods according to the industries which produce them to facilitate a comprehensive study of the relations between the consumption patterns and the industrial structure. But this method is not as clear and direct as the first method. Even in the first kind of classification, we use different methods or models to make forecasts.

(a) Forecast scheme 1

Suppose readjustment of the price system is basically completed in 1990. In this scenario, food prices would register substantial rises, followed by articles for daily use, and stationery and recreational articles; the price of clothing would also go up. Other categories are not taken into consideration because of their small shares. Concrete price index forecasts are shown in Table 4-6.

Table 4-6

HYPOTHETICAL FORECAST OF PRICE INDEXES
(1980=100)

	Food	Clothing	Articles for daily use	Stationery and recreational articles
1980	100	100	100	100
1990	140	108	120	122
2000	150	112	124	124

Table 4-7

FORECAST OF THE CONSUMPTION PATTERN

%

	1980	2000		
		Low level	Middle level	High level
Food	61.4	51.4	50.5	49.1
Clothing	18.3*	17.9	18.1	18.3
Articles for daily use	7.0	14.1	14.6	15.4
Stationery and recreational articles	2.7	5.9	6.2	6.5
Books, newspapers, and magazines	0.6	1.7	1.8	2.0
Miscellaneous	10.0	9.0	8.8	8.7

*The portion of consumption spent on clothing in 1980 is a bit too high. It was 16.8 percent in 1982.

Table 4-8

FORECAST OF CONSUMPTION PATTERN

%

Item	1981 (real)		2000		
	Urban residents	Rural residents	Urban residents	Rural residents	National average
Food	55.66	59.7	46.0	50.0	49.6
Clothing	14.79	12.3	14.5	13.3	13.4
Articles for daily use	18.46	10.2	21.5	15.7	16.3
Fuel	2.12	5.6	1.4	3.2	3.0
Housing	1.55	9.8	2.5*	12.0	11.0
Non-commodity expenditures	6.42	2.4	14.1	5.8	6.7

(Taking average per-capita annual expenditures on consumption as 100%, the table is calculated in terms of the constant prices of 1981)
* Taking into consideration the commercialization of housing, the expenditure on housing will rise to 10%.

In this forecast, we suppose three kinds of income levels, i.e., the average actual income per capita grows at the annual rate of 4.5 percent, 5 percent, and 5.5 percent respectively. The forecast is made at low, middle, and high levels, with the average consumption tendency estimated to be 95 percent. The forecast of the consumption pattern is as follows.

(b) Forecast scheme 2

This scheme forecasts the proportions of expenditures on food, clothing, articles for daily use, fuel, housing, and non-commodity expenditures to the people's average per-capita expenditures on consumption. This forecast is shown in the following table.

The proportion of urban residents' expenditures on food to their total expenditures will drop from 56.66 percent in 1981 to 46 percent in 2000. This percentage falls within the category of a relatively well-off life according to the Engel coefficient. However, compared with the corresponding period in other countries (with an average per-capita national income of 1,000 U.S. dollars), it is still 3-10 percent higher. This is because our country provides subsidies for medical services, education, transportation, rent, grain, oil, and other staple food. If these subsidies are included, the proportion of expenditures on food will fall below 43 percent. The proportion of expenditures on food in the rural areas will drop below 50 percent from 59.7 percent.

After the housing of urban residents is commercialized, rent will be raised to include depreciation charges and management, maintenance, and insurance fees. The state will no longer issue housing subsidies. This amounts to adding to the wages of workers and staff a part of the subsidies for the cost of housing construction; the remainder will be borne by the consumer. By the year 2000, the proportion of urban residents' expenditures on housing to their total expenditures will rise to 10 percent from 2.5 percent.

(c) Forecast scheme 3

we have studied the trend in the development of consumption patterns on the basis of the people's level of income, conditions of resources, population growth, and the development of

Table 4-9

FORECAST OF CONSUMPTION PATTERNS

(%)

Item	1981	2000
Food	59.3	45.4
Clothing	16.8	19.5
Durable consumer goods	10.1	18.3
Furniture	1.4	1.0
Chemical products	2.8	2.9
Railway transport	0.3	0.3
Communications, post and tele- communications	0.8	0.9
Housing	1.6	2.4*
Electricity	0.4	0.6
Coal	1.0	0.7
Petroleum	0.2	0.1
Science, education, culture and public health	3.2	3.8
Service	2.1	4.0
Total	100.0	100.0

*Commercialization of housing is not taken into consideration.
The above table is calculated in terms of the constant prices of 1980.

production. With the opening up of broader areas in the production of consumer goods, people's lives will become richer and more colorful. We attempt to describe these changes in 13 areas as shown in the following table.

The Chinese people's diet structure will undergo certain changes in the future. The proportion of staple foods will decline noticeably, while that of meat, dairy products, eggs, vegetables, and fruit will go up. With the development of the food industry and the steady expansion of food processing, the amount of all kinds of instant food, semi-finished products, and finished products will increase.

The portion spent on clothing will rise from 16.8 percent in 1981 to 19.8 percent in 1990. From then until 2000, the absolute expenditure on clothing will go up, but the proportion will remain unchanged. Expenses on clothing will expand rapidly in the near future, but after a certain period, it will be outstripped by a growing demand for durable consumer goods and for spending on cultural life.

In the midst of this trend of consumption, absolute expenditures on furniture and chemical products will grow, but their proportions of consumption will remain basically unchanged, while the momentum of growth in expenditures on durable consumer goods in both absolute amount and in their proportion of the whole will last until the end of this century.

The proportion of spending on housing will maintain an upward trend because the living area of urban and rural residents will increase substantially. If commercialization of housing is put into effect, the increase will take place on a larger scale. The proportion of expenditures on housing forecast here is widely disparate with that of Scheme 2 because the calculations of housing expenditures are different. Housing expenditure here refers to the rent of urban residents and the charges for the maintenance of houses of rural residents, while that of Scheme 2 refers to the rent of urban residents and the expenses for housing construction of rural residents.

The proportion of expenditures on science, education, culture, public health, and services will all increase. However, the latter will rise faster.

2. Selection of the consumption pattern

The three schemes of consumption pattern have in common a high proportion of the total expenditure spent on food. This is the conclusion drawn by most specialists. However, a small number of specialists, particularly a few young scholars, submitted another scheme.

They maintain that the proportions of spending on food and agricultural products are two components of the consumption pattern that contradict each other most acutely. A comparative study on the economy of many countries indicates that in order to achieve a faster development the developing countries with low income must rely on a high degree of development in machine-building, electronics, chemical, new materials, and information industries. These in turn will push forward changes in the industrial structure through technological revolution and the establishment of a consumption pattern wherein the share of food consumption undergoes a relatively rapid decrease so as to support fast economic growth.

These situations call for in-depth analysis. First, the present high proportion of food expenditure is attributable to a booming rural economy; large quantities of agricultural and sideline products are put on the market, while manufactured consumer goods continue to be monotonous in variety, old-fashioned in design, and poor in quality. The gap between agricultural products and manufactured consumer goods leads people to spend more on foodstuffs. Second, at present, food still forms a high proportion in the consumption pattern of some high-income residents, but we cannot simply take this as a basis to speculate on the consumption pattern in the future. Scientific and technological advances are closely related to changes in consumption patterns. In 1965, only 9.5 percent of American families had color TV sets; the ratio in Japan in 1966 was merely 0.3 percent and in the Federal Republic of Germany it was only 3 percent. Although there were vast differences between the consumption levels of these countries at that time, almost all families in these countries had color TV sets 15 years later. Such changes in consumption could not be predicted by relying on cross-section data 16 years ago. Third, we must take into account the possibility of production and supply and the price to be paid. Food consumption is based on the development of crop cultivation, aquatic production, and animal husbandry. The reform of rural policies has brought about swift growth of agriculture in the past few years. From a long-term point of view, however, the growth rate of crop cultivation can hardly exceed 3-4 percent. The annual growth rate of 6 percent in agriculture set in the above scheme will be very difficult to attain. In short, the output capacity of food will grow lower than the gross social product. Whether consumption can adapt itself to this is the key to the question of whether or not consumption and supply can coordinate with each other. This view warrants attention.

To effect a rapid decline in the consumption on food, it is

necessary to make double efforts to open up other areas of consumption, particularly to adopt effective measures to bring about quick changes in the conditions of housing, transportation, and communications and to develop service trades vigorously.

Section 3
Analysis and Forecast of the Industrial Structure

Industrial structure refers to the proportionate relationship between various production departments and their relations of interdependence and mutual restraint. The former refers to how large a proportion the output value of each industrial department occupies in the total social output value, which can be called industrial composition. As industrial composition cannot reflect the complex relations of interdependence and mutual restraint between various industries, we have to study industrial structure by various methods and from different angles.

1. International comparison of the industrial structure.
Comparison of the Industrial Structures of China and Japan
A comparison of the industrial structures of China and Japan indicates the vast differences between the two as shown in Table 4-10. The data about China's industrial structure listed in the table are based on materials provided by the World Bank after price adjustments.

At present, China's agriculture occupies an important place in the national economy, yet it has a low percentage of marketable products and processing rates, and lacks diversification in production. These features are all the more conspicuous when compared with Japan. For instance, the proportion of China's agriculture in industrial composition is almost four times that of Japan in 1965 and more than five times that of Japan in 1975. Judging from the relations between industries, the input coefficient of Japan's agriculture in relation to nine industries was zero in 1965, while China's agriculture was more or less related to all industries. Compared with Japan, the output value of China's forestry, animal husbandry, and fishery production is out of proportion to that of agriculture. It is especially noteworthy that the position of Japan's greater agriculture, which includes forestry, animal husbandry, and fishery in the whole industry, has declined steadily. This is an inevitable result of modernization. In the course of modernization, the position of China's agriculture must be reduced gradually.

A striking difference exists between the light and textile industries of the two countries. China's food industry is backward, and its textile industry makes up a relatively large proportion of total industrial output. Judging by China's national conditions, the proportion of light and textile industries will not decrease notably in this century while that of the food industry will go up.

From Table 4-10 we can see that heavy industry accounts for 27.06 percent of our industrial setup, about 10 percent lower than that of Japan (Japan's proportion was 36.09 percent in 1975). Heavy industry's degree of reliance on all other industries is higher than that of Japan. This is the result of backward equipment and technology and large raw material consumption. The energy consumption coefficient of our chemical industry is 0.3603 (calculated on the basis of figures after price adjustment) while that of Japan was 0.0948 in 1975. Consumption in heavy industry such as the iron and steel, chemical, and building materials industries is much higher than that of Japan in 1975. This shows that technological upgrading in some of our industries has become a crying need.

Comparing the material consumption of various industries, the proportion of power consumption of China's coal industry is 17.06 percent while that of Japan in 1975 was only 1.58 percent; the proportion of power consumption in China's petroleum industry is 3.67 percent while that of Japan in 1975 was merely 0.69 percent. This universal high energy consumption has resulted in a higher energy proportion in our industrial composition than that of Japan. Even if Japan's import of energy is taken into consideration, its energy proportion is still lower than that of our country.

Table 4-10

COMPARISON OF THE INDUSTRIAL STRUCTURES OF CHINA AND JAPAN

Sector	Japan			China
	1965	1970	1975	1981
Agriculture	4.41	2.72	2.66	15.96
Forestry	1.42	0.81	0.55	0.62
Animal husbandry	1.27	1.08	1.12	4.71
Fishery	0.97	0.72	0.72	0.40
Ferrous metal industry	7.13	8.45	7.42	2.85
Nonferrous metal industry	1.26	1.45	1.03	1.17
Power industry	1.71	1.39	1.77	2.83
Coal and coking industry	0.75	0.60	0.78	3.40
Petroleum industry	1.78	1.79	3.03	10.31
Chemical industry	5.81	5.18	4.81	5.63
Machine-building industry	17.42	21.30	18.19	13.83
Building materials industry	2.82	2.52	2.35	2.19
Forest industry	2.66	2.54	2.09	1.39
Food industry	9.76	7.30	7.35	5.89
Textile industry	4.80	3.31	2.51	6.01
Tailoring, leather industry	1.48	1.42	1.26	1.96
Papermaking, cultural, and educational articles industries	3.53	3.98	3.54	1.91
Other industries	3.79	5.17	5.27	2.48
Building industry	11.29	12.17	13.18	8.85
Transport, post and telecommunications	6.33	5.57	8.54	2.82
Commerce, catering trades, materials supply, and marketing	10.10	10.69	11.60	4.92
Total	100.00	100.00	100.00	100.00

Table 4-11

COMPARISON OF PERCENTAGE SHARES OF THE THREE
ECONOMIC SECTORS IN TOTAL NATIONAL INCOME BETWEEN CHINA AND U.S.S.R.

	1965		1970		1975		1980		1982	
	China*	USSR	China	USSR	China	USSR	China	USSR	China**	USSR
National Income Total	100	100	100	100	100	100	100	100	100	100
Primary sector	42.2	22.5	37.0	21.8		16.9	34.5	15.1	35.9	15.4
Secondary sector	30.7	61	40.4	61.5		64	46.5	61.4	42.3	60.9
Tertiary sector	26.2	16.5	22.6	16.7		19.1	19.0	23.5	21.8	23.7

Notes: * China: 1957 figure. ** China: 1958 figure.

Table 4-12

COMPARISON OF LABOR STRUCTURES BETWEEN CHINA AND U.S.S.R.

	1960		1965		1970		1980		1985	
	China**	USSR	China*	USSR	China	USSR	China	USSR	China	USSR
Primary sector	83.5	39	81.2	31	80.8	25	72.1	20	62.5	20
Secondary sector	7.4	32	9.0	36	10.2	38	16.3	39	21.1	39
Tertiary sector	9.1	29	9.8	33	9.0	37	11.6	41	16.4	41

Notes: * China: 1957 figure. ** China: 1952 figure.

The biggest difference in the industrial structures of the two countries lies in the position of the transport, post and telecommunications, commerce and building industries in their respective economies. In this respect, Japan gives a much more important position to these industries. Compared with it, the proportion of transport and post and telecommunications in China's industrial structure is less than one-third that of Japan; commerce, less than one-half; and the building industry, also less than 50 percent.

Comparison of Economic Structures of China and the Soviet Union

The following three tables are a comparative study of the economic structures of China and the Soviet Union.

Table 4-13 shows the ratio between the three sectors for the two countries, with that of the primary sector being taken as 1.

Table 4-13
COMPARISON OF THE CHANGE OF RATIOS FOR THE THREE
SECTORS BETWEEN CHINA AND U.S.S.R.
(Taking the Primary Sector as the Base)

| | Structure of Output Value | | Labor Structure | |
	China	U.S.S.R	China	U.S.S.R
50s–60s	1:0.72:0.62	1:2.71:0.73	1:0.08:0.10	1:0.82:0.74
	1:1.09:0.61	1:2.82:0.76	1:0.11:0.12	1:1.16:1.06
		1:3.78:1.17	1:0.12:0.11	1:1.52:1.36
80s	1:1.34:0.55	1:4.06:1.56	1:0.22:0.16	1:1.95:2.05
	1:1.178:0.61	1:3.95:1.54	1:0.33:0.26	1:1.95:2.05

From the above comparison, the following conclusions can be drawn:

(a) The ratio of output value between the tertiary and primary sectors has basically remained unchanged for China over the three decades, while that of the U.S.S.R. has doubled.

(b) The ratio of output value between the secondary and tertiary industries for China changed from 1.16 in the 1950s to 1.93

in 1985, while that of the U.S.S.R. changed from 3.71 to 2.56.

(c) The ratio of labor structure between the tertiary and primary sectors and between tertiary and secondary sectors changed from 0.10 to 0.26 and 1.25 to 0.78 for China, and from 0.74 to 2.05 and 0.92 to 1.05 for U.S.S.R.

The above comparative study shows the tertiary sector of U.S.S.R. has achieved greater development than that of China either in terms of the transfer of labor force between the three sectors, or in terms of the changes in output value structure.

2. Trends in the industrial structure observed on the basis of data analysis of several countries.

China is a big country with a large population. To make comparisons with other countries, it is best to make use of data from other big countries with large populations. However, owing to the restriction of materials, all the data we use are from smaller countries with the exception of Japan, because complete input-output tables for these countries in the past decades are available.

(a) Comparison of the composition of total output value, net output value and final demand of various industries and trades, as well as the trends of their changes: To facilitate comparison, we divided various production departments into different categories, including manufacturing industry, building industry, agriculture, raw materials industry, energy, transport, and service trades. From the data of several countries listed in Table 4-14, we can see that the proportion taken up by our country's agriculture is higher than that of all other countries, while the proportions of commerce and transport service are lower than some countries. The data for energy and transport service are on the low side even after adjusting for factors such as price and calculation methods.

From the industrial structure of the countries listed in Table 4-14 we can see that their manufacturing industry and service trades make up a large proportion, about 70 percent altogether, while agriculture and the raw materials industry constitute small proportions, about 10 percent. On the other hand, China's agriculture and raw materials industry assume large proportions, about 30 percent, while the proportion of service trades is too low.

(b) The trend of rational development as seen from international comparisons of the sum total and their changes: In the total supply, the proportion of intermediate input shows an upward trend. This demonstrates that with the rising level of industrialization, more indirect technologies are required, the intensity of the processing of products increases year by year, the exploitation of natural resources becomes more difficult, and the technological and quality requirements become higher.

Some people hold the view that with the rising level of industrialization and technological progress, the material consumption per unit product should decline generally, and the intermediate input rate should show a decreasing trend. Actually, the higher the complexity of products, the tendency is greater that treatment of pollution and other factors will keep the intermediate input on an upward trend.

As added value and intermediate input are mutually complementary, the added value rate will show a downward trend in spite of considerable increases in the total output value and the national income with the development of the economy.

The data of various countries also demonstrate that labor productivity and the capital-output ratio will rise with economic development. Higher economic results lie not only in the decrease of input by more importantly in rising labor productivity and capital-output ratio. From the data, we can also see that the proportion of the volume of imports and exports of various countries in their final demand and the proportion of import in the total supply both show an upward trend.

In the economically developed countries, the ratio of import products being used as intermediate products manifests a declining trend. For instance, most of the import products of Japan and Norway are used for final consumption, but a considerable share of import products of Mexico and South Korea are re-exported after processing. But in recent years, the proportion of import products of these countries being used as intermediate products has remained stable.

The data also show that the rate of average per-capita share of fixed assets is generally going up.

Table 4-14   COMPARISON OF THE INDUSTRIAL STRUCTURES OF SEVERAL COUNTRIES

	Japan 1980 (billion yen)		Norway 1969 (million krone)		Mexico 1975 (million peso)		Yugoslavia (dinar 1972)		China 1981 (hundred million yuan)		China 1980 (hundred million yuan)	
	Amount	%	Amount	%	Amount	%	Amount	%	Amount	%	Amount	%
Manufacturing industry	242.2	43.5	44,764	41.4	216,023	35.4	215,140	44.7	4,280	56.4	2,492	28.9
Agriculture, raw materials industry	16.1	2.9	7,341	6.8	54,512	8.9	75,925	15.7	2,064	27.2	3,026	35.1
Building industry	55.3	9.9	9,386	8.7	46,112	7.5	63,802	13.3	729	8.0	707	8.2
Energy	14.8	2.7	3,527	3.3	42,779	7.0	22,363	4.6	622	6.9	500	5.8
Transport	37.3	6.7	15,837	14.6	49,959	8.2	27,770	5.8	234	2.6	354	4.1
Service trades	191.5	34.4	27,213	25.2	201,486	33.0	76,051	15.8	530	5.8	1,457	16.9
Total	557.2	100.0	108,069	100.0	610,874	100.0	481,150	100.0	9,083	100.0	8,622	100.0

Notes: *Cited from the China Statitics Yearbook (1983), in which the manufacturing industry includes implicitly service trades.

** Cited from the World Bank report on China's structural changes and the possibility of growth and the choice of growth schemes. The standards of statistics are different from those of the China Statistics Yearbook.

Although the proportion of intermediate input to the total amount of supply of various countries has risen in a number of years, the rate has been very slow. Generally, the intermediate input coefficient fluctuates between 0.3 and 0.4 (only that of Japan reached 0.5147 in 1970). China's intermediate input coefficient in 1981 was 0.502. We are of the opinion that China's high intermediate input ratio is the result of high raw material consumption per unit product. Our energy consumption, for example, is three to four times higher than that of many advanced countries. If price differences are taken into account, the material consumption per unit product will be still higher. With the deepening of the reform of the economic structure and the adjustment of prices, it is estimated that the intermediate input ratio will drop for a certain period, which will result in better economic performance. After 1990, the intermediate input ratio will begin to go up gradually, in keeping with the international trend.

Correspondingly, the elastic value of the increase in the national income compared to total output value will continue to increase for a certain period and will be in keeping with the international trend after 1990.

3. Projection of the industrial structure.

(a) The trend of changes in the industrial structure: The average per-capita GNP of the Chinese people in 1980 came to 290 U.S. dollars (calculated in terms of the average exchange rate to the U.S. dollar in that year). It is expected that by the year 2000, China's average per-capita GNP will be about 954 U.S. dollars.

That is to say, in the entire period of the forecast, China will be in a period of transition from low-level income to a middle-level income. The experience of the economic development of many countries in the world shows that this is a period in which the industrial structure will undergo marked changes, and the pace of industrialization will quicken. The result of our forecast indicates that the industrial structure of our country will go through great changes in the next 20 to 50 years. To achieve the goal of quadrupling the gross output value of industry and agriculture and the GNP by the end of this century, changes in the industrial structure are essential.

The industrial structure and consumption patterns cannot be studied in isolation because relations of interaction and mutual coordination exist between them. In China's economy, we have had the experience of low consumption and inadaptability between the consumption pattern and the industrial structure. One of the important reasons for this is the failure to give attention to coordinated study of the overall arrangement for consumption patterns and the industrial structure. Long-range consumption patterns play an obvious restricting and guiding role to the industrial structure, and different consumption patterns can lead the industrial structure in directions favorable or unfavorable to bringing the national strength into full play. Therefore, rational adjustment of consumption patterns must be given an important place in making long-term plans for development.

Our forecast of China's economic structure in 2000 is shown in Table 4-15. Between 1980 and 2000, a number of our economic sectors will develop faster than the average growth rate of the entire economy. These include the infrastructure elements of power, building materials, building, transport, and post and telecommunications industries; the light industries with high output value, such as food, tailoring, papermaking, and other industries; as well as machine-building and chemical industries and commerce and service trades. Some sectors will develop slower than the average growth rate of the entire economy, including agriculture and the petroleum and coal industries. All in all, infrastructure, manufacturing industries, and service trades will develop faster, while agriculture will grow at a slower pace. This conforms to the changes in the industrial structures of most countries.

As various industries have different growth rates, their proportions to the total social output value and the national income also undergo corresponding changes. We have made a rough comparison between such changes and the trend of changes abroad in Chart 4-1. The data about our country in 1980 and that of the typical low-income big countries and typical middle-income big countries are directly quoted from reports of the World Bank.

Table 4-15

PROJECTION OF CHINA'S INDUSTRIAL STRUCTURE

	1980		2000		
	Output value (100 million yuan)	%	%	Times over 1980	Average growth rate in 20 years in %
Agriculture	2,235	25.9	19.4	3.2	6.0
Ferrous metallurgy	334	3.9	3.1	3.5	6.5
Nonferrous metallurgy	139	1.6	1.4	3.7	6.8
Electricity	189	2.2	2.1	4.7	8.0
Coal	160	1.9	1.4	3.2	6.0
Petroleum	290	3.4	2.5	3.1	5.9
Chemical industry	565	6.5	7.8	5.1	8.5
Machine-building industry	1,122	13.0	15.7	5.2	8.6
Forest industry	105	1.2	1.0	3.6	6.6
Building materials	196	2.3	3.0	5.7	9.1
Food	612	7.1	7.5	4.5	7.8
Textile	725	8.4	7.4	3.8	6.9
Tailoring and leather	181	2.1	2.7	5.6	9.0
Papermaking, culture, education	182	2.1	2.5	5.1	8.5
Others	168	1.9	2.1	4.7	8.1
Building	748	8.7	9.3	4.6	7.9
Railway	81	0.9	0.9	4.1	7.3
Transport, post and telecommuni-cations	150	1.8	2.3	5.5	8.9
Commerce	440	5.1	7.4	6.2	9.5
Total	8,622			4.3	7.5

The situation in 2000 is based on our forecast.

The present state of our country's industrial structure is much different from that of other developing big countries, either with a low-level income or with a middle-level income. This is strikingly manifested in the following facts: the proportions of China's manufacturing industry and infrastructure as part of the gross domestic product are far higher than that of other countries with

Chart 4-1. Proportions of Various Economic Sectors in Gross Domestic Product

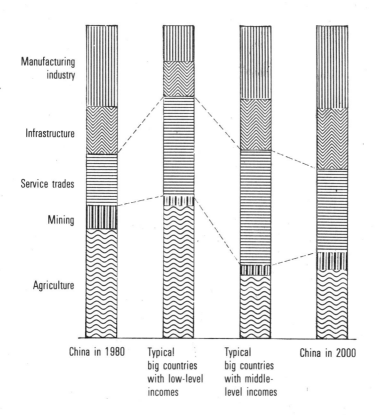

similar levels of income, and they approach and even surpass those of big countries with middle-level incomes; agriculture makes up a high proportion of the gross domestic product, similar to that of big countries with low-level incomes; service trades account for a very low proportion of the gross domestic product, about 16 percent, while that of the big countries with low-level incomes is 33 percent and big countries with middle-level incomes 38 percent.

From the comparison, we can see that by the year 2000 China's industrial structure will improve somewhat, and the proportion of service trades will increase considerably while that of agriculture will go down. This industrial structure will meet the demand for changes in consumption levels and the corresponding consumption patterns in the coming years before the turn of this century. It will guide the national economy to achieve sustained, coordinated growth and help realize the target of quadrupling the gross output value of industry and agriculture on the basis of improved economic returns.

(b) The relations between various industrial departments: The degree of balance between supply and demand of various kinds of products is a yardstick to measure whether or not the economic structure is rational. In our study, we have coordinated the long-term and immediate interests to a certain extent by using long-term plans to guide annual optimum overall balance. There are different standards indicating rationalization of the economic structure. Our belief is that when the supply and demand of the products of various industries strike maximum balance, the economic structure is rational. For a rational economic structure, the nominal prices of the products of various industries should not have big differences. We have attempted to explore the degree of rationalization of the industrial structure by examining deviations from the nominal prices. Using this as a gauge, we find that the trend of development of our industrial structure is gradually becoming rational.

The deviations from the nominal prices of various industries and their changes reflect changes in the strain of these industries. For instance, the nominal prices of railways and communications services have kept rising, particularly in the Seventh and Eighth

Five-Year Plan period. It will not be until 2000 that they will come down somewhat. This is an indication that the restraint of transport on China's economy has become very serious. As railway construction requires a long construction cycle, no tangible results will be achieved in the second decade unless investment is increased in the first decade. However, the demand for railway expansion cannot be fully met because of a shortage of funds in the first decade. Therefore, attention should be given to using the development of highways, waterways, and telecommunications to relieve some of the pressure on railway transport. As the construction of highways, waterways and post and telecommunications projects requires shorter cycle than railway construction, increased investment in the later period of the Seventh Five-Year Plan and the Eighth Five-Year Plan can augment the capacity in these fields in the later period of the Eighth Five-Year Plan and the Ninth Five-Year Plan. Accordingly, an increase in comprehensive transport capacity should be taken into consideration.

4. Some general conclusions on future structural changes of the economy

By analysis and synthesis of the preceding sections, also through collecting opinions from various experts and institutions, some preliminary conclusions can be drawn of the prospects of future structural change:

(a) Towards the year 2000, the power, chemical engineering, machine-building (including electronics), construction and building materials, food, transport, post and telecommunications, paper-making, clothing making and leather processing industries will have a relatively higher growth rate than average.

(b) The structural change will take place by stages. Since the power, transport and ferrous materials supply have already become bottlenecks in economic life, in spite of the lower linkage coefficient of the former two sectors, they should be developed with priority at the current stage. The metallurgical industry should not be taken as the leading sector. Due to the increase of import of steel in recent years, this sector should be developed at the current stage in order to avoid excessive deficit in foreign trade. But it should have a lower growth rate than average in terms of long-term development.

(c) Agriculture, as an essential component of the primary sector, is generally decreasing in its share in the process of development. Due to the huge population of the country, this sector should always receive primary attention. Therefore, a moderate growth rate should be kept for it.

(d) Although the textile industry is a declining traditional sector throughout the world, a moderate growth rate should still kept for it due to its importance in China's structure of export trade at present.

(e) First priority should be given to machine-building and electronics industries. We agree with the idea that developing countries that currently absorb 85 percent of China's machinery exports, will probably remain an important market. Substantial increases in machinery exports to industrial countries are possible. Energetic efforts should be devoted to raising the quality and production capacity of the machine-building and electronics industries to manufacture complete sets of equipment.

(f) Over the past few years, China has imported a large amount of motor vehicles. Efforts should be made to develop the country's production capacity to produce more motor vehicles to substitute imports. Moreover, it is important for the production capacity of motor vehicles to adapt to the development of infrastructure facilities, particularly a well-developed highway network, which is essential in promoting commodity exchange and the development of the rural areas and mountainous regions.

CHAPTER V
CHINA'S INDUSTRIAL POLICY

Section 1
Why the Industrial Policy Attracts Worldwide Attention

The report to the 13th National Congress of the Communist Party of China pointed out, "The historical task to be addressed in the course of expanding the productive forces during the primary stage of socialism is to achieve industrialization and to commercialize, socialize and modernize production. In its economic development, China is faced with the dual task of concentrating on a traditional industrial revolution and at the same time trying to catch up with the new worldwide technological revolution." We should study and formulate an industrial policy suited to China's national conditions in the light of this historical task.

With the deepening reform of the country's economic structure and the implementation of the open policy, the study of the industrial policy has become a more urgent problem. This is because the industrial policy is an important means to achieve economic modernization and embodies a whole set of economic policies. To have a clear idea of the role of the industrial policy, it is necessary to analyze the course of industrialization in the world.

Although the concept of industrial policy came into wide use in various countries of the world only in the past two decades, its basic ideas appeared in the eighteenth century when modern industry was in an embryonic stage of development. From a developing point of view, industrial policy is the general term for all policies of the state designed to promote the course of industrialization. Industrial policy is a policy of government intervention in the market. Whether the market needs intervention has been a controversial issue during the course of industrialization in capitalist countries. Even in the United States with its free market economy, the struggle between laissez-faire ideas and calls for government intervention has existed for a long time. In fact, the policy of government intervention, or the industrial policy, has existed in varying degrees in all countries with market economies, the United States being no exception. This is because even in the early stage of capitalism it was discovered that market prices are important and effective in regulating supply and demand over a short period, but market signals are ineffective for enacting policies for medium-and long-term development. International experience has testified to the imperfection of the market mechanism. Relying solely on market forces cannot solve the problem of structural changes and will adversely effect the optimum distribution of resources. Recognizing the defects of the market has led to an understanding of the rationality of government participation in pushing ahead the changes of the industrial structure and in giving guidance to the market. However, government intervention must comply with the demand for optimum distribution of the resources and help promote competition. The industrial policy took initial form in the 1950s and 1960s. In the course of practice, the ways to deal with the industrial policy have steadily improved. Since the 1970s, it has attracted increasing attention from various countries. The present international trend of structural adjustment and formulation of the industrial policy is attributable to several reasons.

First, Japan's success has aroused worldwide attention. Japan's post-war industrial policy has been a basic means to achieve the strategic objective of catching up and outstripping the industrial powers in Europe and America by fostering the development of strategic industries during different periods. Japan has achieved remarkable success in switching from labor-intensive production to capital-and technology-intensive production and then to the turning out of high-tech products. It has advanced dramatically and emerged as the second largest economic power and the number one creditor country in the world. These accomplishments are inseparable from its enforcement of a correct industrial policy.

Second, the international trend toward structural adjustment and the formulation of industrial policy has been prompted by the need to seek a new method of macro-economic management. Since 1970s, Western countries have come up against numerous economic difficulties. The Keynesian theory of management, which used to serve as the mainstay of their economic policy, has gradually become ineffective. To seek a means or a bridge to integrate development with reform and macro- with micro-economic management is a common problem in world economic life. Some Western economists stated explicitly that the industrial policy is the link between macro- and micro-economic management and a way to free the Western countries from their policy straits. They regard the industrial policy as a revolutionary, new trend.

Third, the situation is influenced by the new worldwide technological revolution. Under the impact of this revolution, Western countries are generally confronted with the task of structural readjustment. Their relative superior positions will change with the mastery of high technologies. The experience of various countries shows that the government's industrial policy is of paramount importance to the development of high-tech industries. This urges people to show more interest in the industrial policy.

Fourth, the trend is stimulated by the United States' need to get over its economic difficulties. Faced with fierce competition from Japan and Western Europe, the United States has run up increasing deficits in foreign trade and is confronted with heavy pressure from the domestic financial deficit. Accordingly, the experience of Japan's industrial policy which has led to the development of various industries has drawn the attention of American economists and government officials. The attempt of the United States, a country with a free market economy, to resort to the means of intervention has attracted people's attention to the industrial policy.

Fifth, the structural readjustment and the adoption of the industrial policy is urged by the need of the developing countries to catch up. After World War II, many developing countries had mapped out a strategy for catching up with and surpassing the developed countries. However, most countries failed in their efforts to carry out the strategy and had to make some adjustments. The experience of a small number of countries which succeeded in the attempt by drawing up industrial policies have arrested people's attention. All economically backward countries have the strong desire to catch up with the developed countries by drawing on their experience of success and importing their funds and technology. The primary condition for success is to set a correct target, formulate a corresponding industrial policy, and have the ability to carry through the policy.

Sixth, a change is required by the need of the socialist countries to carry out reform. The reform being carried out in the socialist countries is one of the major trends in the world today. In the course of reform, efforts have been made to explore the means of indirect control, the means of economic management, and the means of integrating development with reform. The industrial policy is an important means to this end.

Section 2
The Concept and Definition of the Industrial Policy

What is "industrial policy" after all? We have found many interpretations and after comparative studies have set forth our own views.

(a) Industrial policy is the sum total of all government policies concerning industries. "Industrial policy refers to all state statues and policies related to industries." "Industrial policy is the general term of the policies of the state or government, which, to achieve certain economic and social aims, take the whole industry as direct object and through their protection, fostering, adjustment, and improvement of the whole industry, actively or passively participate in the production, operation, and business activities of a certain industry or enterprise, and directly or indirectly intervene in the forming of the commodity, service, and fund markets as well as the market mechanism."

(b) Industrial policy is a plan or the government's guidance plan for the market. As the industrial policy embodies target demands, it can be called the policy of target fixers. It is a plan guiding the market to attain certain targets. "Industrial policy is a policy encouraging or discouraging investment in certain industries."

(c) Industrial policy is a remedial policy adopted by the state to make up for the deficiencies of the market mechanism. "Industrial policy is a policy adopted in the face of a failure of the market mechanism in the field of the distribution of resources."

(d) Industrial policy is the policy adopted by backward countries to catch up with and outstrip the developed countries. "Industrial policy refers to the whole set of policies adopted by one country to strengthen its industries when it lags behind or is likely to lag behind other countries." "Industrial policy is a policy designed to increase the competitiveness of domestic products in the international market."

(e) Industrial policy is a policy of industrialization. "Industrial policy includes all the policies which promote the course of industrialization and which are in the interest of the developing countries attaining a level similar to the European and American countries in the course of industrial development." "Industrial policy is a whole set of policy measures stimulating the transfer of more resources to industrial departments."

(f) Industrial policy is the general term of all kinds of policies of government intervention in economic activities. "Industrial policy is regard as a policy of intervention designed to speed up the growth of certain industries and handle other declining industries. It is usually called the policy of 'selecting the winner and exposing the loser." "Industrial policy is designed to attain economic and non-economic targets by intervening in the distribution of resources among the industries or in the organization of the industries."

(g) Industrial policy is a policy adapted to the development of various stages of industrialization. The scope and substance of the industrial policy change with the passage of time. The objectives, policy measures, and characteristics of various stages are different.

(h) Industrial policy is the supreme policy of economic development. "The industrial policy of post-war Japan is the supreme policy for Japan's economic development. It controls to a large extent the formulation and implementation of Japan's monetary, financial, foreign trade, and foreign exchange policies."

(i) Industrial policy is the policy integrating development with reform. "Industrial policy is a policy that integrates development with reform, planning with market, and macro-economic management with micro-economic management."

(j) Industrial policy is a comprehensive policy system taking development as its aim and reform as a guarantee and involves coordinating the means of control and regulation such as price, taxation, money, finance, foreign trade, foreign exchange, and planning. The formulation of a correct industrial policy can integrate development with reform organically and keep the economic development strategy in step with changes in the model of the economic development.

Roughly, the industrial policy is formed of four policies. First, the policy concerning the industrial structure which is a series of policies adopted by the government to promote the development of key industries and newly rising industries and to revitalize declining industries. Second, the policy regarding industrial organization which has as its chief aim to solve the problem of the behavior of enterprises in the market or to maintain the normal market order for the development of a commodity economy. Thus, the principal part of the policy concerning industrial organization is manifested as the "policy of public economy," and its core is to protect the market mechanism and to make enterprises more competitive. The policy concerning industrial organization has two basic principles: to unleash yet prevent excessive competition and to bring into full play the role of large-scale production. Third, the policy of industrial technology, which enables technology and the products of industries to catch up with the first-rate level of the world and formulates the targets and methods for importing and developing new technologies. Fourth, the policy governing the relations between domestic industries and international industries, which includes policies concerning export, international competition, and international division of labor.

Section 3
The Significance of Studying and Formulating the Industrial Policy

The contradiction between total supply and total demand is an important problem restraining China's economic development. The report to the 13th National Congress of the Communist Party of China pointed out, "To bring about steady economic growth on the basis of improved economic results, we must try to maintain a rough balance between total demand and total supply...." "The overall economic balance is closely related to the economic structure. Only when this balance is achieved on the basis of a rational structure can good macro-economic results be attained." There are several solutions to this problem. One is to curb demand and another is to increase supply. The industrial policy aims at improving supply steadily and giving guidance to demand through readjustment of the economic structure to bring about a rough balance between the two.

The formulation of a correct industrial policy will not only help in the rational arrangement of resources (manpower, finance, materials, foreign exchange, etc.) and promote the the rationalization and modernization of the industrial structure but will also help invigorate micro-economic activities, give correct guidance to the behavior of enterprises, make industrial structure, product mix, and consumption patterns adapt to one another, and bring about a balance between total demand and total supply. It is a matter of paramount importance which has a vital bearing on the sustained, stable, and coordinated development of China's economy and the smooth progress of the economic structural reform in the years to come.

China has set forth many important principles in regard to economic development and some of them involve the question of industrial policy. However, the lack of systematic considerations and supporting reform measures made it impossible to attain the expected results. Thus, systematic investigations and study and formulation of a system of industrial policies have become a matter of pressing necessity.

Through successful rural reform and a series of urban reforms, China's economic structural reform has entered a new stage of stable development. To push ahead the reform, it is necessary to work out an industrial policy suited to the country's conditions on the basis of the accomplishments in construction and reform in the past decade. The industrial policy can coordinate various means of macro-economic control, help realize the optimum distribution of resources, and increase labor productivity by invigorating the enterprises. Consequently, an analysis of the existing conditions of China's industries and the study and formulation of an industrial policy suited to China's conditions are of great practical importance and are dictated by the need to develop and reform.

The means of China's macro-economic management is now shifting from mainly direct control to mainly indirect control. This shift is a profound change. It signifies a change from the predominance of a mandatory product economy to that of a planned commodity economy; a change from control mainly by indexes to management mainly by policy; and a change from stressing growth rates to stressing economic returns. Industrial policy is an important medium of guiding micro-economic activities by means of indirect management.

The study of the industrial policy is dictated by the need to develop a socialist commodity economy and to further planning and reform. Indirect control mainly depends on policy, i.e., creating a macro-environment by means of a set of policies so that micro-economic activities will develop according to objective demands. The industrial policy which embodies these demands is the nucleus of this set of policies.

The control and management of investment remains an

important problem in China's present economic activities. The way to solve this problem is to push forward the reform of the investment system, exercise control over the total demand of investment, and successfully control the sources of investment in light of changing conditions. This requires the adoption of the industrial policy to guide the flow of investment and promote the rationalization of the industrial structure so as to realize the transformation of an old economic system to a new system and push ahead the reform.

The study and formulation of the industrial policy is also dictated by the need for a coordinated development of China's economy, science and technology, and its society and the need for ensuring a steady, sustained economic growth. The perfection of the industrial policy and the modernization of the industrial structure cannot be accomplished in one stroke. It is a process of constant change and development and thus requires a long-range development strategy. A correct development strategy necessarily makes demands on the adjustment of the economic structure to promote economic growth as well as the country's development. The industrial policy is an important means to fulfill these demands.

The formulation of the industrial policy is further dictated by China's need to open to the outside world and strengthen its competitiveness in the world. The study and formulation of the industrial policy will foster a sense for international competition allowing us to catch up with the developed countries. This is competition involves not only the development of production but also the quality of products, the operation of all industries and enterprises, and the management level and efficiency of the government departments. All this is ensured by the industrial policy.

The study and formulation of the industrial policy is a new approach to explore a new model for China's socialist development, because the industrial policy integrates construction and reform, embodies the demands for different stages of development, helps in the fulfillment of plans and the development of the market, and has legal functions. In short, the industrial policy promotes the optimum distribution of resources. As the report to the 13th Party Congress pointed out, "To rationalize the structure of production and the organizational structure of enterprises and to achieve the optimum distribution of resources, we should give play to market forces and free competition. But we should also rely on the state to formulate appropriate policies in this connection and to use such economic levers as price, finance, taxation and credit for intervention and regulation, thus ensuring that reform serves to promote the healthy development of the economy, which in turn will help to create a better economic environment for reform. In this way it will be possible to combine development with reform, planning with the market, and macro-control with micro-flexibility, and to take a new direction in the work of planning." Therefore, the industrial policy we study is a new concept combining development with reform, which is of great importance in promoting the modernization of the country.

Section 4
An Analysis of the Present Condition
of China's Industries

To meet the needs of development and reform, the State Council's Research Center for Economic, Technological and Social Development joined efforts with the various ministries and commissions to launch a study of the industrial policy. In April 1987, they submitted a preliminary report which gives the following analysis of the present conditions of China's industries.

(a) A sign for the better appeared in China's industrial structure during the Sixth Five-Year Plan period. Investigations conducted in a number of provinces and municipalities showed that the effect produced by the demand pattern on the industrial structure increased enormously, which illustrates the active role played by the introduction of market mechanism; that the changes in production increased with the rising level of income, demonstrating the accelerated growth of the country's economy; and that the growth rates between agriculture, light industry, and heavy industry have become more harmonious, creating conditions for the steady development of China's economy.

(b) Looking from the angle of continued development of production over the years, the general pattern of the industrial structure has improved but the irrationalities underlying the industrial structure which were formed in the past and which affected economic growth have remained basically unchanged. These find expression chiefly in the following facts: basic industries are lagging far behind; the processing industries have developed too fast, and their patterns in various provinces are similar; the idling and straining of productive forces exist side by side, and the shortage and overstocking of resources exist simultaneously; and the situation in which most of the country's exports are primary products has not improved much.

(c) In the early period of the Sixth Five-Year Plan, China enforced the policy of giving priority to light industry. At the same time, capital construction projects were drastically curtailed. There was a surplus in the production capacity of heavy industry and the basic industries, which created material conditions for the fast growth of the processing industries. The processing industries have maintained a great momentum of growth. The rises in the people's income, particularly that of the farmers, enlarged the capacity of the domestic market, giving fresh impetus to the growth of the processing industry. Meanwhile, more agricultural population moved to industrial and other non-agricultural jobs and urbanization was accelerated. These applied heavy pressure on the basic industries requiring that they synchronize with or develop in advance of other industries. In other words, the advance coefficient should be a positive value.* In fact, however, the leading coefficient of the basic industries was a negative value throughout the Sixth Five-Year Plan period. The lagging basic

---

* The advance coefficient of basic industries equals the ratio between the growth rate of the output value of basic industries and that of the total social output value minus one. Positive value indicates that the growth rate of basic industries is faster than that of the total social output value. A converse situation is indicated by a negative value.

industries not only affect the steady growth of the economy at present but also produce an adverse influence on the development within this century and even thereafter. The basic industries of all countries in the world which have achieved successful development advance ahead of other industries.

(d) The various provinces of our country have for a long time sought to set up an independent economic system and paid little attention to lateral economic ties. The industrial structure of various provinces is identical. While the basic industries are weak and the general efficiency is low, processing industries have grown steadily and universally. The changes in the industrial structure of various provinces and municipalities are very similar, either. Their comparative advantages in resources and productive forces have not been effectively brought into play. The industries they have vied with each other to develop are mainly those that produce TV sets, refrigerators, washing machines, motor cars, and other products that enjoy ready markets. As the production of these commodities relies heavily on imported materials and parts and they are sold at higher prices, it is difficult to sustain this type of production. Moreover, the Chinese people's demand for durable consumer goods is irregular, mass production of these commodities often lead to overproduction. This was the case with the production of wrist watches and sewing machines. It is thus highly important to our country's development in various areas that we enter into mutual cooperation on the basis of regional division of labor while bringing each area's comparative advantages into full play.

(e) In the industrial structure itself, the situation of shortages existing side by side with overproduction is very serious. Judging by statistical analysis, shortages and lagging production are more apparent. But looking closer at the industries, regions, and enterprises, we see that on the one hand there are shortages, but on the other there is overstocking. This situation is quite obvious between and within various departments, industries, and enterprises. The coexistence of shortages and overstocking has aggravated the imbalance of the industrial structure.

(f) The course of modernization of the industrial structure is incompatible with economic growth. Over the past few years since the introduction of reform and the adoption of the open policy, structural changes have taken place in the demand for raw materials and parts and components in both production and consumption. With the development of the economy, the demands for such products will be huge and lasting. Accordingly, the development of domestic basic industries should catch up with the demand instead of relying entirely on imports. International experience also shows that earning foreign exchange by exporting primary products to sustain development is a road that leads nowhere. The fundamental solution lies in promoting the modernization of the industrial structure.

(g) Some scholars attribute the irrationality of the industrial structure to the irrationality of the institutional mechanism which makes it difficult for industrial production to consciously regulate its product mix in both quantity and quality. However, this problem should be considered by combining development with reform. In the course of reform, it is necessary to make clear the target of adjustment of the industrial structure, tighten the means of guiding the flow of extra-budgetary funds, draw up regional policies and export strategies, employ the means to realize optimum distribution of resources, and set forth measures to increase overall economic results. To do all these, it is necessary to have sufficient understanding of the importance of the rationalization of the industrial structure to economic development.

(h) Further analysis of the industrial structure will touch on the industrial organization. It is one of the key problems of economic development. Since the commencement of reform, encouraging changes have taken place in China's industrial organization. Economic associations set up by different departments, regions, and ownerships have provided valuable experience for exploring the forms of movement of the essential factors of production and the restructuring of the industrial organization. However, it must be noted that utterly irrational situations still exist in the industrial organization. These are manifested in the following facts: Both the degree of concentration and the degree of dispersion of the industrial enterprises are poor, and it is difficult to fulfill the demand of large-scale production on the basis of specialized association; the enterprises have poor capacity for innovation and inadequate technological reserves; the operations of enterprises are passive and on a short-term basis; and new enterprises adopt old technologies, existing enterprises find it difficult to make technological innovations, and it is hard for enterprises to enhance their capacity for international competition.

(i) The most serious defect of China's industrial organization lies in its lack of concentration and dispersion based on specialized association. There are two major tendencies in the industrial organizations of developed commodity economies: the concentration of production, i.e., the essential factors of production are increasingly concentrated in specialized large enterprises; the dispersion of production, i.e., the essential factors of production are scattered among miniature and extra-miniature enterprises which cooperate with large enterprises. In the midst of these two major tendencies, the network of industrial organizations in developed commodity economies take shape. The enterprise's ability to compete, its achievements in scientific research, its cultural level, and its employment are all involved in this elastic network. Japan, for instance, is not only known in the world for its establishment of giant enterprises, its small enterprises are equally characteristic. Its number of small enterprises employing 1-29 people accounts for 91 percent of the total number of enterprises, their employees make up more than one-third of the total number of employees, and their output value accounts for 34 percent of that of light industry and more than 20 percent of that of manufacturing industry. The number of small enterprises employing 1-4 persons makes up 51.3 percent of the total number of enterprises. These small enterprises do not exist in isolation but form groups of enterprises with big enterprises as their nuclei.

In this respect, there is a wide gap between China and the developed countries. The degree of concentration and dispersion of industry is determined when the enterprises are set up. The expansion of the scale of enterprises is mostly the result of increased investment in their expansion, instead of the movement and realignment of the essential factors of production. Most of China's big enterprises are comprehensive instead of specialized factories. There is a vast difference between the scale of production of big enterprises and their economic scale. Statistical data from around the world show that as the large-scale production of the auto industry has marked economic results, the production of motor vehicles, especially automobiles, in a country is highly concentrated. The degree of concentration indicates the proportion of output of the largest or several large auto factories in the total output of motor vehicles of the whole country. Generally, the concentration ratio of one factory reaches 45-50 percent, two factories 75-80 percent, three factories 85-90 percent, and four factories as high as 95 percent. In China, however, the concentration ratio of the three largest auto factories reaches only 59.7 percent. China had more than 80 commercial auto plants in 1984, surpassing the total number of commercial auto plants in the United States, Japan, Germany, France, Britain, and Italy. The specialized cooperation of the essential factors of production is also very poor in our country. Small enterprises also tend to become all-embracing. The number of ultra-miniature special industrial enterprises is very small. It is necessary to invigorate the enterprises through reform in order to increase labor productivity. But more importantly, it is necessary to invigorate enterprises by promoting specialized division of labor. In this way we can achieve the notable result of increasing macro- economic effect. This is one of the major objectives of the reform as well as a way to realize the · movement of the essential factors of production and the realignment of the productive forces.

(j) Another serious defect of China's industrial organization is its poor ability to make innovations and its inadequate technological reserves. The real motive power of economic development lies in the innovating activities of enterprises. It is the innovating enthusiasm of seeking new materials, developing new products, opening new markets, and exploring new methods of management that is the inexhaustible source of economic growth.

Under the present economic system in China, it is difficult for enterprises to innovate and they are often short of technological reserves.

Our investigations conducted in 18 provinces and municipalities show that the basic reason for the massive overstocking of consumer goods in 1986 lay in the gap between the productive capacity of enterprises and the residents' consumption tendencies. An important reason leading to this situation was the enterprises' insufficient motive power in making technological developments. Another important reason was the repetition of technological achievements among enterprises. The key scientific and technological problems being tackled in some factories were often problems that had already been solved in other factories. This problem should be solved by changing the behavior of enterprises.

(k) The so-called market behavior of enterprises generally refers to the strategic actions taken by enterprises to achieve higher profit targets and higher commodity selling rates. It usually includes the selection of the price, quality, product, investment, and distribution strategies by enterprises. In the attempt to invigorate enterprises, the problem of the short-term market behavior of enterprises crops up, which makes it difficult for enterprises to achieve optimum scale and innovation.

It must be noted that the short-term tendency of enterprises, market behavior is closely connected with their passive operation. Owing to the difficulties in streamlining their administrations and delegating the decision-making powers to lower levels, the behavior of enterprises is essentially restricted by administrative intervention. The prices of the products turned out by the enterprises are decided by the government. The investment, commodity selling rate, and quality of the products are based on the policies of the governments at various levels and the departments in charge of them. In such a passive position, it is impossible for the enterprises to consider their strategies. From the investigations in 18 provinces and municipalities, we can see clearly the logical connection between small-scale investment and investment in light and processing industries on the one hand and the short-term tendency of the enterprises on the other hand.

(l) According to the theory of enterprise life cycle, all enterprises go through the natural "physiological processes" of birth, development, maturity, and withering away. The stages of birth and development of an enterprise are its period of youth, while the stages of maturity and withering away represent its period of old age. The age of an enterprise is determined by its ability to handle market competition and its ability to innovate. Young enterprises and industries should be protected, while aging enterprises and industries should be eliminated. Only in this way can we ensure the vitality of the entire economy.

A typical feature of Chinese enterprises is that they have the dual characteristics of a young enterprise and an aging enterprise. When an enterprise is set up, it starts with old technology, old products, and old methods of management. Thus, it can hardly become competitive and develop the ability to innovate. At the same time, it wastes large quantities of resources.

(m) All the irrationalities of the industrial organization find expression eventually in the stagnation of resources. Although China has various characteristics of a "shortage" economy, the shortages are actually only a superficial phenomenon. The fundamental problem lies in the fact that the flow of the stagnant resources is severely restricted, thus leading to the coexistence of shortages and overstocking. In the absence of a moving mechanism such as amalgamation of enterprises and bankruptcy, normalization of the scale, innovation, behavior, and growth of enterprises is very difficult. Therefore, the fundamental way out for the rationalization of the industrial organization and the industrial structure lies in solving the problem of the movement of the essential factors of production.

(n) The problems existing in the industrial structure and the industrial organization are the sources of the irrationality of our present structure of industrial economy and the difficulties we encounter in creating a realized economic environment. These problems are attributable to China's traditional system and the problems in the distribution pattern arising from changes in construction policies over the past 30 years. We should work out a rational industrial policy based on reform because it is a feasible way to promote the rationalization of the structure and the optimum distribution of resources.

Section 5
The Characteristics of a Sound Industrial Policy

The sound industrial policy should have the following characteristics:

1. Systematic character—The industrial policy touches on a wide range of areas. Its formulation and implementation are in fact a gigantic and complex example of systems engineering. The main policy and supporting policies constitute the industrial policy systems. In the course of study, the complicated mutual relations of development and reform need systematic analysis; the industrial structure, consumption patterns, investment patterns, and foreign trade patterns require comprehensive analysis; the employment patterns, personnel patterns, technological patterns, and educational structure require interrelated analysis; the present policy and future policy and the policies of the central government and the local governments also need systematic analysis.

2. Dynamic character—The formulation of the industrial policy is related to the changes in domestic and international conditions and the changes in market competition. It is necessary to study and improve the industrial policy constantly. Therefore, the study itself is dynamic. The advantages of a country or region have always been relative. For an open economy, the relative interests always change. It is necessary to follow such changes closely and adjust the industrial policy in good time. Objectively, the industrial policy has a dynamic character.

3. International character—We study and fix our national and regional industrial policy while China and the world are changing and developing. The trend of development of new technologies offers us opportunities and poses a challenge to us. Worldwide structural adjustment and the new trend of international division of labor requires that various countries, in

their study of the industrial policy, take into consideration the developing trends in the international industrial structure.

4. Compressible character—In the course of industrialization, the industrial policy can help shorten the time required for its realization. This is the reason why the industrial policy has arrested worldwide attention. In drawing up and implementing the policy, we should take note of this point. We should shorten the time required for industrialization, compress the course of industrialization, and speed up modernization.

5. Practical character—The study of the industrial policy is not simply an academic study but is closely linked to development and reform. For this reason, it is necessary to integrate the leading industries and strategic industries and satisfactorily arrange the echelons of industries. Giving attention to changes in the industrial structure, we must support the leading industries in terms of funds, labor force, and technology and at the same time set about fostering the strategic industries. All industrial structures have structural inertia. Changing and adjusting the industrial structure require a long-term strategy, from strategic industries to leading industries. It cannot be accomplished overnight. Its success depends on whether the forecast is correct or not and whether the measures taken are correct or not. At the same time, the relations between the leading industries and strategic industries must also be taken into account.

6. Forecast character—Correct forecasting is the foundation for the formulation of a scientific foundation and realistic industrial policy. For example, two major economic think tanks of South Korea, the Korean Development Institute (KDI) and the Institute of Industrial Economy, are engaged in the study of the industrial policy, making timely analysis and forecast of the changes in the industrial structure and providing a foundation for scientific policy making.

7. Differentiating character—Differences are indispensable to policy. The policy of finding a single solution to all problems is in contravention to the essence of the industrial policy:

(a) Differentiation between industries must be made from various angles. The primary, secondary, and tertiary industries are different. The trades in various industries are different. The product mix in the same trade is different. For the same product there are different scales of production and different economic results.

(b) The various provinces and municipalities are different, the coastal areas and inland areas are different, and the urban and rural areas are different. To map out a successful industrial policy, it is necessary to proceed from the actual conditions of economic development. Japan has a small and narrow land. The differences between various regions are relatively small and the conditions of enterprises in various regions are relatively balanced. Nevertheless, there are still considerable differences between various regions. China has a vast territory and the development of various regions is extremely unbalanced. For this reason, it is all the more necessary for different regions to have their own industrial policies to bring their advantages into full play and promote the economic growth of the whole country. Under the unified policy guidance of the central government, the local governments of various provinces, autonomous regions, and municipalities directly under the central government should have the authority to draw up certain special industrial policies for the administrative areas under their jurisdiction. The formulation of regional industrial policies will be instrumental in arousing the initiative of the localities and will avoid the defect of uniformity in industrial policy. China is a unified country and a country the different parts of which have their own unique characteristics. Accordingly, China's industrial policy should reflect this diversity. Only on this basis can an effective national industrial policy be formulated. The national comparative advantage is shaped on the basis of the comparative advantages of various localities.

(c) There should be differences in terms of time and stages. The major time divisions refer to the primary, middle, and higher phases in the course of industrialization. The standards for selecting the leading industries in different stages should be different. The newly rising industries today may become leading industries tomorrow. There should be several echelons of leading industries arranged in the order of time sequence. The adjustment of the industrial structure should ensure continuity over time.

8. Different level character—The industrial policy system has different levels. To study the industrial policy, it is necessary to analyze the relations between different levels of the policy. The industrial policy system has also a network relationship.

(a) The national industrial development is a synthesis of regional industrial development as well as the result of the execution of the whole set of industrial policies.

(b) The upper-level regional industrial development is the synthesis of the lower-level industrial development. The upper-level industrial policy provides guidance to the main direction and principles of industrial development of the lower level, but its implementation must rely on the corresponding policy and measures formulated by the lower level. In other words, the policy of the upper level sets the principles for that of the lower level but cannot replace the policy of the lower level itself.

(c) The level-by-level management and responsibility under unified planning and the attempt to find a single policy solution for different problems at the lower levels will impede the localities from giving full play to their advantages. It is necessary to have a guidance plan covering lower-level development. The State Planning Commission has a corresponding guidance plan covering the whole society. This is a new demand put forward by development and reform on planning work as well as summing up experience of the previous stage of development. Only when we have a guidance plan for the whole society can we analyze whether or not the arrangements within the budget and the state plan are appropriate.

(d) It is necessary to make overall arrangements and to have unified planning, standards, principles, guidelines, and open policies and to establish a unified socialist market. Only with overall arrangements and distinctive policies can the advantages of the localities be brought into full play and can a unified socialist market be established.

9. Information character—The industrial policy can employ the following policy measures: (a) Indirect guiding policy, including taxation, customs duties, and trade restrictions; (b)

Direct control policy, such as the quota system; and (c) Information providing policy, including various policies transmitting information between industries or enterprises or providing places for information transmission; all kinds of government examination meetings, long-term plans, and prospects for the industrial structure worked out by the planning departments, such as demands on statistics, trade, data, and policy transparency—all these mean to give guidance to the behavior of enterprises.

10. Indirect character—The industrial policy is a policy guidance and is essentially an economic measure. There must not be too much government intervention, particularly administrative intervention. Otherwise, industrial policy will become ossified. Such a situation happened in South Korea resulting in negative economic growth. With increasing independence of enterprises and the enhancement of their strength, the industrial policy should be switched to strengthening macro-economic control and reducing direct policy intervention.

Section 6
Preliminary Suggestions for China's Industrial Policy

We have advanced the following initial proposals on the basis of our study.

1. We must acquire a clear understanding of the strategic thinking of using the industrial policy to link up development with reform

Our central idea is to unify reform and development and coordinate a series of major relations in our economic life with the targets set in the industrial policy.

The industrial policy we put forward is aimed at setting up an economic system that combines competition with intervention. For this we have to work out a guidance plan with the industrial policy as its nucleus. Our purpose is to seek a dynamic balance and the optimum distribution of resources on this basis. We propose to set up the industrial policy in two stages. In the first stage, while the internal relations of the industrial structure are still irrational and the market mechanism is imperfect, we should set up a rationalized structure and organizational system using mainly domestic resources to ensure sound economic growth. On the condition of ensuring structural rationalization, the stress of the policy should be placed on the rationalization of the industrial organization which promotes the movement of the essential factors of production and aims at the realization of production at proper scale. We should coordinate macro-economy with the policy concerning industrial structure and guide enterprise flexibility with the policy of industrial organization.

In the second stage, while the micro-economic foundation has been improved and the general pattern of the industrial structure has been straightened out, we should design the optimum orbit for the operation of our industrial structure in light of an exchange of international resources and against a wider international background in order to achieve a perfect industrial structure and an industrial organization that will bring high economic returns.

2. The industrial policy in the first stage should lay stress on policies concerning industrial structure and industrial organization

At present, China's economy has entered the stage of making preparations for a major take-off. To ensure sustained, stable, and coordinated economic growth, it is necessary to adopt the following policies concerning the industrial structure: the policy of improving the basic structure and increasing the ability of supply of essential factors of production; the policy of building the system of distribution by local leading departments and the national leading departments; the trade policy placing emphasis on the cooperation of international industrial structures.

CHAPTER VI
CHINA'S REFORM OF THE ECONOMIC STRUCTURE

Section 1
The Progress of the Economic Structural Reform

1. New developments in theory

The Third Plenary Session of the 11th Central committee of the Communist Party of China held at the end of 1978 marked the start of China's reform of its economic structure. So far, the reform has scored momentous successes and has injected new vitality into socialism. To speed up and deepen the reform, it is necessary to have a deeper understanding of the nature of the reform of our country's economic structure.

In June 1981, the Party Central Committee summed up the historical experience since the founding of the People's Republic and advanced the thesis that China is still in the primary stage of socialism. The Resolution of the Central Committee of the Communist Party of China on Guiding Principles for Building a Socialist Society With Advanced Culture and Ideology adopted in 1986 further expounded this thesis. It pointed out, "Since our country is still in the initial stage of socialism, we must apply the principle of distribution according to work and develop the socialist commodity economy and competition. Also, for a long time to come, we shall develop varied sectors of the economy, always ensuring the dominant position of the public sector, and we shall encourage some of the people to become prosperous first, before the objective of common prosperity is achieved." This set the tone for the reform of our economic structure. All the reforms we have carried out, including the development of varied sectors of the economy while ensuring the dominant position of the public sector and permitting the existence and development of the private sector are all determined by the actual conditions of the productive forces in the primary stage of socialism. Only in this way can we promote the development of the productive forces.

The 12th Party Congress pointed out that the socialism we are building is socialism with Chinese characteristics. This is a principled requirement for the reform of our country's economic structure. The Decision of the Central committee of the Communist Party of China on Reform of the Economic Structure adopted by the Third Plenary Session of the Party's 12th Central Committee said explicitly that our socialist economy is a planned commodity economy based on public ownership. This is a scientific summation of the socialist economy, a momentous development of Marxism, and the theoretical basis for our economic structural reform. It represents a new development on several major theoretical questions. First, it has negated the outdated idea which pitted planned economy against commodity economy, and has established the theory that a socialist economy is a planned commodity economy. Second, it has discarded the obsolete concept that a planned economy is nothing but mandatory planning and made clear the new idea of gradually reducing the scope covered by mandatory plans, switching to establishing the dominant position of the guidance plan, and fully making use of the market mechanism. Third, it has shattered the outmoded idea that ownership is inseparable from management power and ushered in the ideas that administration should be separated from management and ownership from management power, and that the methods of enterprise operation should be diversified. By shaking off the shackles of old ideas, the decision laid the ideological foundation for further carrying out the reform and the open policy.

2. Two stages of the reform

In the first stage, the stress of the reform was on the rural areas. The main aspects of the reform were the gradual popularization of the household-based contract responsibility system characterized by linking remuneration with output, which aroused the farmers' enthusiasm in production, the abolition of the people's commune and restoration of township government, and the raising of the purchasing prices of agricultural products by wide margins which promoted commodity exchange between urban and rural areas. While rural reform was in progress, useful experiments on urban reform were also conducted in various fields including expanding the decision-making powers of enterprises.

The decision on economic structural reform adopted at the Third Plenary Session of the 12th Party Central Committee, held in October 984, marked a new stage of reform with the stress laid on cities. In the second stage, the emphasis of rural reform was placed on solving the relations between the peasants and the state, readjusting the industrial structure of the rural areas, and promoting an all-round development of the rural economy on the condition of ensuring a steady increase in grain output. In the cities, the stress is placed on enhancing the vitality of enterprises by setting up a comprehensive market system through supporting reforms in planning, finance, taxation, price, banking, as well as the labor and wage system.

3. Rural reform

With regard to reform in the rural areas, the people's commune system, which integrated government administration and economic management, was abolished; the household-based contract responsibility system with remuneration linked to output was gradually popularized throughout the country; and the relations between the farmers and the collective was rationalized. By the first half of 1987, the household-based contract responsibility system was introduced for 180 million farming families, accounting for 98 percent of the national total.

As the state adopted a series of policies, such as substantially raising the purchasing prices of agricultural and sideline products, readjusting the rural production structure, and encouraging the development of a rural commodity economy, the rural economy developed rapidly. The purchasing prices of agricultural products were raised by 20.1 percent in 1979 and further raised by 8.1 percent in 1980. The reform aroused the enthusiasm of the country's 800 million rural population. The output of grain and cash crops, such as cotton and oil-bearing crops, increased year by year. There was an overall development of agriculture, animal husbandry, sideline production, and fishery, which provided the market with ample commodities. In the total output value of agriculture, the proportion of forestry, animal husbandry, sideline occupations, and fishery reached 51 percent. Rural enterprises employed more than 76 million people, accounting for 21 percent of the total labor force in the countryside. The average net per-capita income in the rural areas rose from 134 yuan in 1978 to 424 yuan in 1986. After adjusting for price rises, the farmers' actual income increased 2.6 times in eight years. Along with economic growth, cultural, educational, scientific and technological, and public health undertakings all developed considerably in the rural areas.

Beginning from 1985, the state monopoly for purchasing and marketing of agricultural and sideline products was abolished and the state no longer sets mandatory purchasing quotas to the rural areas. Instead, the new policy of state purchase by contract was introduced. After fulfilling the purchase contract, the farmers can sell their remaining farm produce freely in the market.

Reform in the rural areas is now deepening. With the development of the commodity economy, more of the labor force is switching to industry, commerce and service trades. Land has begun to concentrate in the hands of big farmer households specially engaged in crop cultivation. On the basis of family operation, the farmers are voluntarily developing associated households or cooperative operations in a small way in the fields of processing, transport, and marketing of agricultural and sideline products. Cooperation in supply and marketing, circulation of funds, and credit undertakings are developing in the rural areas.

4. Readjustment of the ownership structure
Under the prerequisite of continuously upholding public

ownership, the structure of ownership has been readjusted. The proportion of non-state sectors of the economy involved in industrial production has risen from less than 19.2 percent to 31.3 percent, and their proportion in the total amount of retail sales has shot up from 9.5 percent to 60.6 percent. Sixty percent of the state-owned small commercial enterprises are leased out to be operated either by individuals or collectives. Experiments have been conducted in a number of state-owned medium-sized and small enterprises with the joint-stock economy. Through these reforms, China's ownership relations have broken through the uniform model of ownership by the whole people and formed a new pattern with the public sector of the economy playing the dominant role and with diverse forms of ownership existing side by side and developing together.

5. Reform of industrial enterprises

To smooth out the relations between the state and enterprises is a basic problem which must be tackled by the reform. The reform of the enterprise management system, aimed at increasing the vitality of enterprises, was carried out through gradually expanding enterprises' power of independent management. Documents issued by the State Council clearly set forth the responsibilities, powers, and interests of enterprises as relatively independent commodity producers and managers. They make it clear that the enterprises have the decision-making power to select a manner of operation; make arrangements for production, supply, and marketing; control their own funds, labor personnel, wages, and bonuses; fix the prices of their products; and form lateral associations. In 1986, a series of measures were taken to dissolve a number of state administrative organs which held control over the enterprises and to ban unjustifiable allocation of financial and other quotas to enterprises. All these created conditions for enterprises to carry out independent operations, bear responsibility for their own profits and losses, and seek development on their own resources.

In 1987, new advances were made in deepening the reform. The contract managerial responsibility system in various forms was introduced with the emphasis laid on invigorating large and medium-sized state enterprises. In accordance with the principle of separating ownership from management power, the enterprises were run by the managerial staff with their ownership belonging to the state. Contract management is a transitional form in the reform leading to standardization and will be further developed in the future. While introducing the contract system, a series of supporting reforms have been made in the internal management mechanism and external environment of the enterprises.

In the course of the enterprise reform, the state has adopted measures to promote lateral economic association of enterprises. By the end of 1986, there were more than 32,000 economic associations of various kinds in the country.

6. Reform of the planning system

In the reform of the planning system, the scope covered by mandatory plan and unified prices gradually reduced, and the market mechanism began to play a regulating role. By 1986, products covered by the mandatory plans of industries under the control of the State Planning Commission had been reduced from 120 kinds to 60 kinds, the varieties of materials under the unified allocation of the state had decreased from 256 to 26, and commodities under the planned control of the Ministry of Commerce had dropped from 188 kinds to 23 kinds. The proportions of commodities for which floating prices were introduced were: agricultural and sideline products, 65 percent; industrial consumer goods, 55 percent; and capital goods, 40 percent.

7. Reform of the commodity circulation system

Reform in the field of circulation saw the monopolized operation of state commercial enterprises changed, a vast number of collective and individual commercial establishments set up, rural trade fairs opened in cities, and state monopoly of the purchase and marketing of manufactured goods for daily use abolished. In the reform of the circulation system, various forms of economy and methods of operation and diverse channels of circulation were developed. At the same time, a number of wholesale agencies of state commerce were changed into economic entities, and their vitality enhanced.

In the field of circulation of capital goods, the means of production entered the market as commodities and many capital goods service companies and trade markets were set up. Many kinds of means of production can be freely purchased in the market today. Trade markets for rolled steel and other means of production have been set up in a number of large and medium-sized cities. In 1986, about 30 percent of rolled steel and more than 40 percent of cement were sold by the manufacturing factories themselves. About 25 percent of the coal produced by large state coal mines were sold through their own channels.

In terms of the purchase and marketing of commodities, the system of level-by-level distribution according to administrative regions has been changed. Trade centers were set up according to economic zones which have broken down the barriers between regions and now allow them to serve the whole country. This represents a step forward towards the establishment of a unified market.

8. Reform of the wage and bonus system

The reform of China's wage and bonus distribution system began with adjustment of wages and the restoration of the bonus system of a compensatory nature, thus enlarging the decision-making power of enterprises on bonus distribution. The income of the workers and staff began to reflect their labor contribution. After 1984, various forms of experimental reforms were carried out on the distribution of wages and bonuses in enterprises. Some enterprises practiced the method of linking up the growth of the total amount of wages with the taxes and profits delivered by enterprises to the state, tying the total amount of wages to economic performance. These measures began to break up the egalitarianist and "iron-rice-bowl" practice that characterized wage distribution in the past. The state has imposed a bonus tax to control the growth of wage funds.

9. Reform of the profit and taxation system

Before 1983, China's state enterprises practiced the system of keeping a portion of their profits by themselves. Aside from the portion retained by the enterprises according to fixed proportions, all the profits made by the enterprises were delivered to the state treasury in the reform of profits. In 1983, the first step was taken to replace profit delivery with tax payment. The profits to be delivered to the state were changed into payment of an income tax at a rate of 55 percent, with the rest remaining unchanged. Beginning from the fourth quarter of 1984, the second step was taken—the profits made by large and medium-sized state enterprises were delivered to the state in the form of income tax and regulatory tax, and after paying the taxes the enterprises retained all the remaining profits. After the second-step reform of the taxation system, the average profit retained by each enterprise showed an increase of 80 percent compared with the first-step reform. Before 1978, the enterprises practiced the system of unified income and expenditure, and they retained a very small proportion of profits. By 1986, after years of expanding the decision-making power, the profits retained by the enterprises increased to 42 percent of all profits they made, making it possible for them to seek self-development.

Aside from those enterprises for which the system of substituting tax payment for profit delivery was introduced, a small number of large and medium-sized enterprises were chosen to experiment with the system of retaining all the profits left after fulfilling various kinds of contract targets of profit delivery to the state. In the past few years, the Ministry of Railways, the China National Petrochemical Industrial Corporation, and other departments have carried out the input-output economic contract responsibility system with satisfactory results.

10. Price reform

China's price system has been in a distorted state over a long period of time. The following measures have been taken in the price reform. First, the purchasing prices of agricultural and sideline products were raised. In 1985, the purchasing and marketing prices of meat, poultry, and eggs were raised, and restrictions on the prices of non-staple foodstuffs such as vegetables, fish, etc., in the cities were lifted. At the same time, the government issued subsidies to urban residents for non-staple food price rises. In this way, the price parities between industrial and agricultural products gradually became normal. Second, control of the prices of small commodities for daily use and service and repair trades were gradually relaxed. Enterprises were allowed to fix prices themselves or to negotiate prices with the buyer. The prices of more than 1,000 small commodities were allowed to fluctuate. In 1987, the proportion of industrial products with prices fixed by the state was reduced to 40 percent of the total sales of industrial products. Third, a double-track price system was practiced in regard to iron and steel, motor vehicles, coal, and a number of machinery and electrical products. In other words, products for which state quotas were set through state plans adopt state prices, while the portion above the quotas are allowed to be sold by the enterprises themselves at floating or market prices. Fourth, high quality products were sold at higher prices. Fifth, the prices of some products were adjusted upwards or downwards. Thus China's price system has changed from unified prices set by the state into the coexistence of state prices, fluctuating prices under state guidance, and market prices. The price reform has to be pressed forward and the force of the market must be brought into fuller play. At the same time, the inflation rate has to be kept relatively low.

11. Reform of the monetary system

We have set up a monetary system with the central bank, or the People's Bank of China, as the leading force, and the various special state banks, such as Agricultural Bank of China, the Industrial and Commercial Bank of China, the Bank of China, and the People's Construction Bank of China as the backbone, along with the coexistence and division of labor and cooperation of non-banking financial institutions, including insurance companies, trust and investment companies and credit cooperatives. Under the supervision of the central bank, active efforts have been made to develop all kinds of financial institutions, permitting competition and some overlapping of their businesses. Monetary markets have been opened and expanded, which included the inter-bank loan market, commercial bills market, as well as short-term bond market and other short-term fund markets. At the same time, a long-term fund market, or capital market, was set up on a trial basis.

With changes in the distribution pattern of the national income, funds for economic construction now mainly come from credit channels instead of financial channels. The proportion of newly increased bank deposits in the national income rose to 14.7 percent in 1986 from 2.3 percent in 1978. Of the total funds flowing to production, construction, and circulation in the whole country, those provided by banks increased to 68.4 percent in 1986 from 23.4 percent in 1978, and those provided through state revenue dropped to 32.6 percent from 76.6 percent. The monetary system is playing an important part in economic development.

12. Experiments on the comprehensive reform of the urban economic structure

Since October 1984, experiments on the comprehensive reform of the urban economic structure have achieved further advances. By the first half of 1987, the number of cities conducting comprehensive urban reform had increased to 72. Sixteen medium-sized cities carried out experiments on reform of government organizations and five cities on housing commercialization. The experiments were aimed at strengthening the multiple functions of the major cities in economic development, opening up all kinds of commodity markets, especially money markets, technology markets, and labor service markets, and turning cities into open, multi-functional, and socialized and modernized economic centers.

Section 2
Deepening of the Economic Structural Reform

To conduct further reform in the future, we should correctly sum up and draw on the experience in the past few years and proceed from the realities of the present stage of reform. Reform has brought vitality and hope to China's economy, but in the course to replace the old system with the new, contradictions and problems are bound to emerge. To deepen the reform it is necessary to make new explorations and new breakthroughs.

The report to the 13th Party Congress said, "At present, our main task in deepening the reform is to change the managerial mechanism of enterprises and, with that end in view, to institute supporting reforms in the systems of planning, investment, allocation of materials, finance, monetary affairs, and foreign trade. In this way we shall gradually establish the basic framework for a planned commodity economy."

1. Difficulties to be overcome in deepening the reform

To make the relations between the state and enterprises harmonious is one of the basic problems which must be solved through the reform. Efforts have been made in this respect in the past few years. The main problem existing at present is that the decision-making power of enterprises, particularly large and medium-sized state enterprises, has not been truly exercised—the budgetary restraint on enterprises has not been strictly carried out and to a great extent the enterprises are responsible only for their profits and not for their losses. The way to solve this problem, as the report to the 13th Party Congress pointed out, is to invigorate "enterprises owned by the whole people by separating ownership from managerial authority." In order to establish a planned commodity economy, it is essential to separate ownership from managerial authority, to give enterprises real power of management, to rationalize relations between owners, managers, and producers, and to protect the legitimate rights and interests of enterprises so that they are able to make their own management decisions and take full responsibility for their own profits and losses. In the course of separating ownership from managerial authority to bring about changes in the operation mechanism of enterprises, it is necessary to handle satisfactorily the relations between the diverse manners of enterprise management and the standardization of enterprise control.

An enterprise should be able to produce, manage, develop,

and invest. The decision-making power should include the authority to perform these duties. Enterprises owned by the whole people (that is, state-owned enterprises) are a long way off from meeting these requirements, and legal guarantees in this respect are yet to be perfected.

The existing price system has to be reformed because it has a serious adverse effect on economic development and structural reform. The irrational price mechanism affects the establishment of the market system, while the rationalization of the price system depends on the development of the market. Eventually the forming of prices has to rely on the market. Price reform affects the vital interests of every enterprises and urban and rural residents. We have to take into consideration the ability of the society to stand the pressure. We have to carry out price reform but must avoid the political risks it may bring about. We have to rationalize the prices yet have to keep inflation under control. This is a difficult task we have to tackle.

Although the reform of the investment system has made progress, the thirst for investment has not been basically changed. This is a big obstacle to the implementation of the strategy of stressing economic returns, raising quality, coordinating development, and achieving stable growth, which must be overcome.

In the future, state investment should be confined to large public utilities, infrastructure projects, and a small number of large key enterprises. The local governments should be responsible for local infrastructure and public utilities. Construction of productive enterprises, in general, should be undertaken with investments by the enterprises or new investment groups. The funds for investments should be obtained mainly through the capital market, and the practice of using funds without compensation should changed completely. Government investment should also be separated from state finance. Foundations or securities companies should be set up to manage the capital instead of controlling it. In this way, state investment will continue to increase. As this problem involves the sharing of power and interests between the state and enterprises, changes in the economic management functions and division of financial power between the central and local governments, as well as changes in the government functions and the division of labor between financial and banking institutions are also hard nuts to crack.

Under the old system, the government mainly relied on three means to manage the economy: the distribution of funds; the distribution of materials; and administrative decrees. Whereas under the new system, that is, the system of a planned commodity economy, the coordination of the production, supply, and marketing of products and the optimum distribution of resources are mainly realized through the market. With the change in its economic functions, the government will no longer manage the production, the supply of materials and marketing of products, as well as personnel and financial affairs of the enterprises, but instead exercise control over the total demand and total supply of the whole society and the formulation of development policies. Accordingly, it is necessary to change the government's economic management organizations. The main efforts should be directed at strengthening the comprehensive departments, supervision departments, and information and advisory organizations and substantially streamlining specialized management organs. Such changes should be made in conjunction with the reform of the political system and require a drastic change in ideas. Thus, they also pose great difficulties.

2. Suggestions for deepening the reform

How to deepen the reform is a question under study. Comparisons should be made to select the best scheme. The following are a few proposals:

(a) The scheme to create an ideal economic environment. Resolute measures should be taken now to reduce total social demand and create a favorable economic environment without inflation as soon as possible; then steps should be taken to speed overall reform of enterprises, price, taxation, finance, monetary, and investment systems;

(b) The scheme of laying a solid groundwork. This scheme

lays stress on carrying out, supplementing, and perfecting the reform measures that have been taken to lay a solid foundation for the next step of the reform;

(c) The scheme calling for strengthening macro-economic management. Under conditions of appropriate centralization, efforts should be made to strengthen macro-economic abilities, whereas the macro-economic control should be matched by a suitable level of micro-economic flexibility;

(d) The scheme of deepening enterprise reform: With the stress laid on the reform of the investment system, corresponding measures should be adopted to improve macro-economic management, to gradually rationalize the relations between the state and enterprises and between the central and local governments, and to push ahead the reform stage by stage.

We should make an analysis and forecast of the relations between the steps of reform and policy coordination in accordance with the guidelines of the 13th Party Congress.

3. Concerning the macro-economy

In the field of macro-economy, several problems warrant our attention. The demand for investment surpasses domestic accumulation, and this calls for strengthening control. The decentralization of finance and the retention of profits by enterprises have reduced the scope of the central finance activity. Overheated investment and bloated consumption have put prices under sustained pressure, and the government has had to resort to overissuance of currency. These are complicated situations which have no simple solution. But answers may be found in the following three aspects:

(a) China's accumulation rate is higher than that of most other countries. If the funds are used appropriately, they can meet the demand for investment in the country. We should promote the establishment of a unified state market, encourage specialized production, and reduce the waste of investment on repetitive construction projects. We should step up the building of power projects and transport facilities and overcome these weak links in the national economy to bring into full play the existing production capacity of enterprises. This is more important than solving the problem of the shortage of funds. We must take steps to prevent the production capacity of newly built industries from growing faster than that of power generation and the construction of transport facilities. Otherwise, the newly added equipment will lie idle.

(b) The ratio between China's taxation and national income is by no means low compared with countries of similar levels of development. If more taxes are imposed on state-owned and medium-sized enterprises, their enthusiasm in production and operation will be adversely affected. The government's financial situation can be improved by reducing subsidies to lighten financial burdens and by tax reform to increase tax income.

(c) We should continuously expand the monetary market mechanism and facilitate the accumulation of funds. This will contribute to the increase of investments and help in forming the commodity market. Raising the interest rate can also curb the demand for investment and is in the interest of increasing returns on investment.

(d) The development of the market is of decisive importance to the optimum distribution of resources and to increasing the effectiveness of delegating powers to lower levels. The success in the effort to develop the market hinges on the professional training of managers and entrepreneurs and an improvement in their professional skills—their ability to apply scientific economic regulations, their skills at mastering the policies of investment—as well as the establishment of all kinds of mechanisms related to the development of the market such as offering legal services, guaranteeing the interests of the consumers, and providing market information. The government should have regulatory organs to monitor the functions of the market and supervise the implementation of market regulations.

(e) We should develop a national unified market to expedite the realization of specialized production. First of all, it is necessary to develop transport, communications, and other infrastructure facilities to strengthen the ties between the market and the industries. This requires that the state has a high-level scheme and closely coordinates with the industrial policy. It is necessary to change the present social and political attitude which is favorable to the self-sufficient development of the localities and to set up unified economic regulations and a system which will cover the whole economy. The different market regulations of various provinces and municipalities are unfavorable to the forming of a unified market which is the main source of vitality of the industries.

We wish to point out here that some foreign experts hold the opinion that for macro-economic reasons, it is necessary to limit the scope of tax contracting because of its implications on the government's ability to introduce discretionary fiscal policies. And they also think that decentralization to the local government—another feature of the tax reform—has also reduced the control of the central government over the use of tax policies for macro-economic objectives.

Section 3
The Target Model of the Economic Management System

1. The target of the economic structural reform and the optimum distribution of resources

The Decision of the Central Committee of the Communist Party of China on Reform of the Economic Structure adopted at the Third Plenary Session of the 12th Central Committee affirmed the general orientation and principles of China's economic structural reform. In accordance with these principles, we should design a set of specific target model charts in conformity with this decision. Once the target model is fixed, the question arises as to how to pass on from the existing economic system to the target model. This is an urgent question because only when a practical model of transition is designed and the method of transition is fixed can the target model be successfully realized.

The decision pointed out, "The essential task of socialism is to develop the forces of production, create ever more social wealth, and meet the people's growing material and cultural needs." In other words, the target of our economic structural reform is to promote the high-speed growth of social productive forces.

We believe that the target model of our economic structure should be to create maximum material and cultural wealth, primarily material wealth, with our limited manpower, material and financial resources to meet the needs of the people's demand for an improved standard of living and the sustained growth of the national economy, known in economics as the "optimum distribution of resources."

The distribution of resources refers to all kinds of resources, including manpower, material and financial resources. When the manager of an enterprise makes arrangements for the machines, factory buildings, labor force, and funds that can be used, chooses the raw materials and motive power than can be obtained, and decides on the mix of products and investment projects to pursue, he is distributing resources. When a socialist country draws up long-range and medium-term economic plans and formulates the industrial policy, it is distributing resources. When the state makes use of such economic means as taxation, interest rates, and exchange rates, it is also indirectly distributing resources. Rational distribution of resources, using an equal amount of input to get the maximum output and using the minimum resources to turn out a given output—all these represent optimum distribution of resources.

The concept of the distribution of resources was given attention early in the eighteenth century. For the last 50 years, international economic circles have been carrying on a debate around the question of the optimum distribution of resources. The focus of the controversy lies in whether or not optimum distribution of economic resources can be achieved under the socialist system, in other words, whether or not it is possible for the socialist system to attain an economic efficiency equal to or higher than that of a capitalist market economy. Western bourgeois economists declare that the Western market economy approaches a market of complete competition, and according to the theory of Adam Smith, optimum distribution of resources can be achieved. They argue that under the socialist system, there is no market, it is impossible to have a set of rational prices, and therefore it is impossible to distribute resources and organize production rationally. This argument was refuted by other economists. In 1936, Polish economist Oskar Lange published his thesis *On the Economic Theory of Socialism*. He believed that by adopting the method of "trying again if a mistake is made" in a socialist economy it is possible to find a set of rational prices to make the supply and demand of all products meet and to rationally distribute resources. The debate lasted a long time without any conclusion. And we still face the question: whether or not we can and should include the optimum distribution of our resources as a target of our economic structural reform. This is a question of great importance. The model of economic structure we envisage should be able to achieve this target. We have proved not only theoretically but also in practice that we can have an efficiency equal to and even higher than that of the capitalist market economy.

2. The target model of the economic structural reform

What is the model for the reform of China's economic structure? The decision on economic structural reform adopted by the CPC Central Committee has pointed out the basic orientation. At present, however, it has to be made clear gradually in the course of the reform because many particulars still cannot be fixed. Generally speaking, it will include the following aspects:

(a) It will be a system that integrates the market and the plan, competition and intervention, a system that combines the strong points of the market and the plan, relies on the plan to overcome the ills of the market economy and improve the industrial structure, and depends on the market to make the plan conform more to reality and be more effective.

(b) The enthusiasm of enterprises will be brought into full play. As the enterprises have decision-making powers, most economic activities will depend on decentralized policy decisions.

(c) Planning work will be highly scientific. The coordination of the activities of various sectors will rely on the economic levers, on the means of macro-economic restraint and economic parameters, and on scientific planning and policy to ensure that under the conditions of the rational distribution of resources, the total macro-economic amount and the industrial structure will be effectively controlled, and serious disproportions and waste will be avoided.

(d) The price system will become rationalized, and prices will be established by the market.

(e) The socialist market system will be established which will include not only the markets for consumer goods and the means of production, but also markets for the essential factors of production, such as capital, labor force, technology, information, and real estate.

(f) A national unified market will take shape which will promote specialized cooperation.

(g) On the question of ownership, the structure in which various forms of ownership (ownership by the whole people, collective ownership, and private ownership) coexist with public ownership playing the dominant role must be established. The principle of turning state enterprises into communities in which the state, the collective and the individuals share the same fate should also be affirmed. Whether the joint-stock system will become the main form of ownership of state enterprises remains to be studied and proved by practice.

(h) An indirect control system will be established and the role of finance, banking, and other economic levers will be greatly strengthened.

(i) The separation of the functions of the Party from those of the government, of government administration from enterprise management, and of ownership from managerial authority will all be realized.

(j) The system of democratic management of enterprises will be perfected. A unified, effective, and highly efficient production and management system will be set up in enterprises, and the workers' congress system will be improved.

The projection of the target model of the economic structural reform will be steadily improved with the deepening of the reform.

CHAPTER VII
SCIENCE AND TECHNOLOGY
IN DEVELOPMENT

We have mentioned in Chapter I of this book that "we must make prompt use of the new results of scientific and technological research to develop our economy and technology," because science and technology will play a dominant role in the modernization drive, and the basic concept of our development strategy is "coordinated development of economy, science and technology and society" (see Section 3, Chapter IX). Hence, we shall give a relatively detailed treatment of China's science and technology system and its future prospects in this chapter.

Section 1
Retrospect of China's Science and Technology System

1. Development of the science and technology system since 1949

For more than 30 years, China has had a rapid development in its science and technology system and has established a system of six component parts.

(a) The first part is the Chinese Academy of Sciences. In 1949, it had only 21 research institutes (including social sciences) with only about 200 research workers. In 1984, there were 118 research institutes manned by more than 70,000 staff members, of whom over 44,000 were scientific and technological personnel and more than 3,200 were above the rank of associate professor.

(b) The second part of the system is the scientific research and planning organizations that function under the various departments of the State Council or those on the local level such as the Academy of Agricultural Sciences, the Academy of Geological Sciences, the Research Institute of the Ministry of Railways, the Scientific Research Institute of Petroleum Prospecting and Exploitation, etc. Their main task is to engage in applied research closely related with the needs of the departments and regions of which they are a part.

(c) Research organizations that operate under institutions of higher learning are the third part of the system. In 1949, there were 205 institutions of higher learning. Recent information shows that there are 760 institutions of higher learning with 481,088 scientific and technological research personnel, of whom 356,088 persons are scientists and engineers.

(d) The fourth part of the system is the research organizations run by factories and mines. Their main concern is project-related, involving such areas as production development and construction. Many large factories and mines set up their own research institutions or offices.

(e) The fifth part of the system is the Chinese Academy of Social Sciences. In a modern society, social science plays the critical role in providing data for government policy-making. Development planning has been commonly adopted throughout nearly the whole world since World War II, which allows for a broad discussion of social science research findings and interpretations with the purpose of preparing for and giving greater depth and long-term effects to policy decisions. The Chinese Academy of Social Sciences is a national research center for human and social sciences in the People's Republic of China. It came into being in 1977 as a result of the reorganization of its predecessor—the Department of Philosophy and Social Sciences under the Chinese Academy of Sciences. At the time of its formation, there were 16 research institutes, in comparison to today's 33 research institutes, three research centers, a postgraduate school and a publishing housing. The total number of researchers and staff of the academy at present is 5,000, among whom 3,000 are researchers, editors, technicians, engineers and translators of foreign languages.

(f) The final part of the system is the research organizations for national defense, which concern themselves mainly with newly developed techniques needed for national defense.

2. Achievements of the Science and Technology System

Since 1949, China's science and technology developed rapidly, resulting in many important achievements, such as the development of nuclear and hydrogen bombs, intercontinental missiles, geosynchronous satellites, etc. In 1957, the first "12-Year Scientific and Technological Development Program" was adopted. Our breakthroughs in jet technology, semi-conductor and computer technology, as well as nuclear technology are largely the results of the success of that program. In March 1978, a national conference on science was held by the state and attended by 6,000 representatives. This conference formulated an eight-year plan (1978-85) which singled out eight areas of research as the key sectors: agriculture, energy, materials, electronic computers, lasers, space, high energy physics and genetic engineering.

Information on the current status of natural science is given in Tables 7-1 and 7-2.

Section 2
Experiences and Problems in the Development of the Science and Technology System and the Decision on the Reform of the Science and Technology Management System

1. Experiences and problems

China has been successful in establishing a socialist economy and building up a considerably large contingent of scientific and technological researchers. In addition, it has developed a industrial setup embracing nearly all branches. The country's economic structure has both advantages and disadvantages. On the one hand, the over-concentration of power by the government, the egalitarianist tendency in distribution and rigidity in economic control made it impossible for the science and technology system to meet the needs of the growing production. On the other, the

Table 7-1

RESEARCH INSTITUTIONS OF NATURAL SCIENCE
(Classification based upon research activities)

Item	No. of institutions	Total number of employees	People engaged in research		
			Total	Scientists and engineers	Other types of scientific personnel
Total	4,690	770,416	575,736	231,050	121,000
Agriculture, forestry, animal husbandry, fishery, hydraulic engineering (except hydropower)	1,377	182,364	115,430	37,799	21,219
Industry	1,882	61,067	278,132	104,559	55,696
Geological exploration and survey	61	15,732	12,861	7,048	2,521
Transport, postal and communication service	98	19,371	16,326	7,602	3,541
Construction	103	13,786	11,295	5,089	2,596
Others	1,169	178,096	141,692	68,953	35,427

Table 7-2 CLASSIFICATION OF INSTITUTIONS BASED ON THE NUMBER OF EMPLOYEES

		With more than 1,000 people	With 500-999 people	With 300-499 people	With 200-299 people	With 100-199 people	With 50-99 people	With less than 50 people
Total	4,690	102	229	316	392	868	982	1,801
Under the State Council	622	62	120	116	74	110	79	61
Under provinces, autonomous regions, and muncipalities	3,946	22	75	171	303	740	895	1,740
Under Academy of Sciences Chinese	122	18	34	29	15	18	8	0

structure made it easier for the government to pool all the necessary resources for the fulfillment of its social, economic, as well as scientific and technological development goals.

The "top-down technology push" approach to innovation adopted by the various ministries under the central government and the weakness of linkages between the elements of a complete production life-cycle were the main causes of the inefficient operation of the Chinese science and technology system in the past.

These problems were described briefly in the Decision of the Central Committee of the Communist Party of China on the Reform of the Science and Technology Management System dated March 13, 1985: "However, it must be recognized that the current science and technology management system, which has evolved over the years, suffers serious defects which hamper the gearing of science and technology to economic construction, the rapid transformation of scientific and technological achievements into productive capacity and the full use of the wisdom and creativeness of our scientific and technological departments to meet the objective needs." These are the reasons why we should reform our science and technology management system, and this reform will provide the background of our science and technology policies.

2. Decision on the Reform of the reform of the Science and Technology System

The major contents of the reform of the science and technology management system are in the following three main aspects: reform of the operating mechanism, reform of organizational structure and reform of the science and technology personnel system.

(a) Reform of the operating mechanism entails the reform of the funding system, the development of a technology market and the reform of the planning system for research projects to overcome the defects of relying purely on administrative means in science and technology management.

The reform of the funding system is mainly directed at

changing the financial allocation practice in the past. For quite a long period, the government allocated research funds unconditionally to the research institutes according to the number of their staff, thus creating an indifference to economic consequences on the part of the research community. In view of this situation, the funding system will be reformed in four ways.

First, for a given period of time, funds provided by the central and local governments for scientific and technological undertakings will increase gradually at a rate higher than the growth in regular state revenues in order to encourage scientific and technological development.

Second, for basic research and part of applied research, funds will be provided through research foundations. But for research institutions engaged in technological development activities, the government allocations for the current expenditure of those organizations will be gradually reduced and abolished over a period of five years.

Third, banks are encouraged to provide credit loans for scientific and technological work, and supervise and control the use of such loans.

Fourth, research institutions engaged in important research projects for public good, such as medicine, public health, labor protection, family planning, prevention and control of natural calamities, environmental sciences and other social sciences, and institutions providing certain scientific and technological services, such as information, will continue to receive state allocations with block funding practice.

(b) Reform of the organizational structure

The objective of the reform of the organizational structure is to change the following situations: a disproportionately large number of research institutes are detached from enterprises; coordination is lacking between research, design, education and production; the defense and civilian sectors are separated from each other; and barriers remain between various departments and regions.

Reform of the organizational structure will focus on strengthening enterprises' capability to absorb and develop technology and on strengthening the intermediate links of a production life-cycle system as shown in Figure 3. Emphasis is placed on encouraging partnerships between research, educational and design institutions on the one hand and production units on the other. Detailed suggestions on how to achieve this are as follows:

First, research institutes under the Chinese Academy of Sciences, the institutions of higher learning, the research institutes under the central ministries and local governments should be encouraged to set up various forms of partnerships with enterprises and design units on a voluntary and mutually benefit basis. Some of the partnerships may gradually become economic entities.

Second, some research institutes may develop on their own into enterprises of a research-production type or become joint technology development organizations for small and medium-sized enterprises.

Third, large key enterprises should gradually improve their own technology development departments or research institutes.

Fourth, defense research institutes should create military-civilian partnerships. While ensuring the fulfillment of national defense assignments, they should serve economic construction, accelerate the transfer of technology from the military to the civilian sector and engage energetically in research and development programs for civilian products.

Fifth, collectives and individuals may set up research or technological services on their own. Local governments should exercise control over them and give them guidance and assistance. Profit-oriented institutes of this category are allowed.

(c) Reform of the personnel system

The objective of the reform of the personnel system is to encourage the emergence of a large number of talented people who can put their specialized knowledge to best use. This objective will be realized through four methods.

First, "giving the proper person the proper position" is the best way to use human resources in an organizational society. The old generation of Chinese specialists will be provided with conditions for them to continue to play their role in training qualified personnel and directing research, in writing books, acting as consultants and promoting diverse public activities. A great number of accomplished and vigorous young and middle-aged people will be assigned to key academic and technological posts. Scientists and engineers in their forties and fifties should be encouraged to contribute their full share as a bridge between the older and younger generations. And the young talents should be helped to come to the fore.

Second, in solving the serious aging problems in many of our leading research institutes, measures should be taken to train different types of scientific and technological managers of a new breed who possess modern scientific and technological knowledge and management skills.

Third, the mobility of personnel should be encouraged. Competent people must no longer be made to sit idle and waste their talent. Appropriate scientific and technological policies and preferential measures should be adopted to encourage scientific and technological personnel to work in small and medium-sized cities, in the countryside and in regions where minority ethnic groups live in compact communities. Research and design institutes and universities may gradually experiment with recruiting their personnel by invitation so as to break the so-called "iron-rice-bowl" practice.

Fourth, efforts should be made to improve the working and living conditions of the scientific and technological personnel. The principle of "from each according to his ability, to each according to his work" should be carried out in earnest to oppose egalitarianism in distribution. Proper awards for scientists and engineers should be introduced gradually and effectively. A system of honors and material rewards should be instituted.

(d) Reform of the planning system for research projects

The research projects of national priority will remain under the control of the state planning apparatus, while other activities conducted by the scientific and technological institutes are to be managed by means of economic levers and market regulation so as to enable these institutes to develop an internal impetus and endow them with the vitality to serve economic construction on their own initiative.

3. Main considerations about the educational system

The development of the science and technology system not only calls for solutions to its own problems but also depends on an essential input—the human resources. The Central Committee of the Chinese Communist Party and the State Council of the People's Republic of China jointly convened a national conference on education in May 1985. About 500 leaders of provincial Party committees and heads of educational bureaus under the various central ministries and provincial governments, presidents of some universities and colleges, and distinguished teachers participated. As a result of the conference, the Decision on the Organization and Management of the Educational System was announced on May 27, 1985. The essential heading of the decision are summarized as follows:

(a) to produce more skilled manpower of higher quality;

(b) to implement nine-year compulsory schooling by steps;

(c) to readjust the structure of secondary education and vigorously develop vocational technical education;

(d) to reform the system of college admission and recruitment planning and placement of the graduates, and to extend the autonomy of higher learning institutions.

(e) To strengthen supervision over and guidance to education so as to ensure the successful implementation of the decision.

Section 3
Science and Technology System in Transition

Since the decision was made public, several major steps have been taken for its implementation.

1. Establishment of the National Natural Science Foundation Commission

In order to strengthen basic and applied research and

gradually establish the science foundation system, it was announced in February 1986 that the State Council had decided to set up the National Natural Science Foundation Commission.

The major responsibilities of the commission are:

(1) To prepare and issue project guidelines for basic research and applied research based on the National Science and Technology Development Program, to accept the applications for research projects, to organize specialists of related sectors for project evaluation and to subsidize projects in a selective way;

(2) To provide advisory services for important basic and applied research problems;

(3) To coordinate and direct the assignment of research tasks;

(4) To engage in international cooperation and establish contacts with national science foundations of other countries.

Funds for the commission will be mainly provided by the state budget from the Ministry of Finance. The commission also can accept contributions from units and individuals both domestically and from abroad. The funds are to be used mainly to support the research and management expenses of approved projects; a certain part of the funds are to be used for international cooperation, for arranging scientific exchanges and for supporting the research work of young eminent scholars.

This organization consists of 25 members, all of whom are well established scientists and management experts.

2. Development of the technology market

The development of the technology market is designed to meet the requirement for developing a socialist commodity economy. This new development has opened a fresh way for scientific research findings to be applied to production. The first national conference on technology trade was held in Beijing in March 1986. The five-day session, which was attended by more than 300 representatives from across the country, ushered in a new phase in the development of the technology market, one important content of the reform of the science and technology management system.

Experiments on the reform in fact started several years ago.

For instance, in 1985 more than 3,000 technological trade fairs were sponsored, with a combined business volume of 2.3 billion yuan, three times that of 1984. Again for example, the establishment of a technology market in Liaoning Province quickly expanded the province's technological trade scope. Intermediary technological trade agencies mushroomed, with around 1,000 organizations of different kinds, such as technological development centers, advisory centers and service centers, of which about 500 were state-owned and about 400 were collective or individual ones.

Technological trade can be in many ways, including the transfer of single items, technological training courses, technological information, and research upon entrustment.

3. Establishing closer links between research institutes and rural enterprises

One major step in this endeavor is the launching of the "sparking program," which aims at spreading "sparks" of knowledge and skill to start a "prairie fire" of development in rural China.

The program was sponsored by the State Science and Technology Commission, which has entrusted scientists and engineers with the job of designing simple and low-cost equipment that can produce relatively high economic returns and are easily adaptable to use in the countryside. The program also called for training an army of farmer technicians.

In the first five years covered by this program, efforts will be centered on three aspects of work: designing and putting into mass production of 100 kinds of complete sets of equipment suitable for use in the countryside; building 500 pilot enterprises to demonstrate to rural people the technological progress, the methods of management and the quality control of products; and training 1 million rural school graduates and managers of rural enterprises in various skills.

Section 4

Future Prospects for Science and Technology

1. Science and technology by the year 2000

The prospects for science and technology by the year 2000 were studied through joint efforts of the State Science and Technology Commission, the Chinese Academy of Sciences, the Ministry of Petroleum and several research institutions under different ministries.

Science and technology is a sub-system of the broader economic and social system. It is well known among economists that innovation holds the key to faster economic advance both for the developed and developing countries. It is a natural consequence that nearly all the governments in the world give their greatest attention to science, technology and innovation. Of course, government can play a dominant role in the establishment of a proper science and technology policy by setting priorities, by proper allocation of research and development spending and by strengthening the linkage between the different elements of a complete research-development-production cycle (Figure 1 shows our understanding of research and development as one of the stages in a complete production life cycle). But science and technology policies reflect to a certain degree the specific problems which individual governments face. Here, we shall mention certain roles to be played by the government through the sub-report on science and technology, a part of the study "China Towards the Year 2000," which will also show some of the background of Chinese science and technology policies.

2. Major points of the sub-report

(a) The basic objective of the development strategy for science and technology is to serve the development of the national economy and society, to turn scientific and technological products into useful social production capacity, to promote the transformation of knowledge and technology into economic efficiency, to contribute to the prosperity of the market and to raise the standard of people's material and culture life.

(b) The strategy for scientific and technological development towards the end of this century is based upon two presumptions. First, our country is a developing country with a population of over 1 billion. We have established an industrial foundation of certain scale, but we have not completed our industrialization. Hence, there is plenty of room for the further development of traditional technology and industrial activities. Second, The current worldwide new technological revolution will have a great impact on the development of our country. We have the opportunity to use the new and existing technology of the world to speed up our modernization drive; but we must be aware of the fact that we have a poor technological infrastructure and do not have enough qualified scientific and technological personnel and insufficient financial resources. Thus, there is the great danger that the technological and economic gap between our country and the developed countries will widen.

(c) In view of these constraints, our basic strategy will be to treat traditional technology and high technology as an integrated system. We are going to develop further traditional technology as a whole, but it is necessary also to pay attention to the development of high technology, focusing on using it to reinvigorate traditional technology and existing enterprises. The traditional technology we are going to develop in fact has lost its original sense. What we mean is a technology mix of traditional technology with high technology.

(d) The development of the science and technology will be divided into two stages. In the first stage (including the Seventh Five-Year Plan period and the beginning of the Eighth Five-Year Plan period), we will devote primary attention to the development of traditional technology and industries. At the same time, we will make extensive use of microelectronic technology, which belongs to the category of high technology, to reinvigorate the traditional technology and industries. At the second stage (the second half of the Eighth Five-Year Plan period and the entire Ninth Five-Year Plan period), we will switch our major attention to quickening the development of high technology, while continuing to develop traditional technology and industries.

(e) The detailed policies deprived from the strategy for the development of science and technology towards the end of this century will include the following six aspects:

1) We must stick to the open policy in order to expand import of technology from abroad to accelerate the development of our country's scientific and technological capability.

2) We must execute the policy to reinvigorate existing enterprises. China has now more than 6,000 large enterprises, 400,000 medium-sized and small enterprises and several million rural enterprises. The reinvigoration of these enterprises calls for a huge amount of scientific and technological work. We must guard against the tendency to divorce the development of science and technology from this objective. The use of high technology in the technological upgrading of traditional industries embodies four aspects: using microelectronic and information technology for the technological revamp of the energy, transport and communications industries; application of integrated manufacturing systems; using bioengineering to raise the level of agricultural production, food and pharmaceutical industries; and developing new materials.

3) We must view the development of high technology very seriously to establish the urgently needed industrial sectors in time; we must select a proper leading technology to form a technological gradient group; we must form a multi-strata hierarchical technological structure based on the specific characteristics of various regions, taking into full consideration the imbalance of development among them; and we must stress development research.

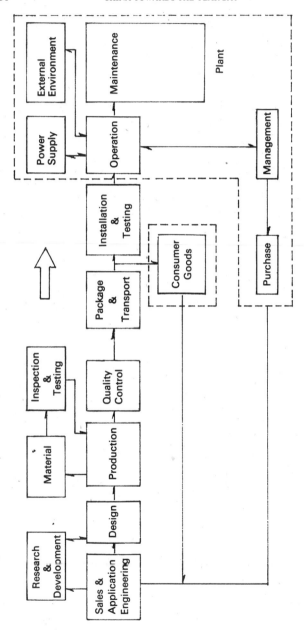

Fig. 1   Complete Research-Development-Production Cycle

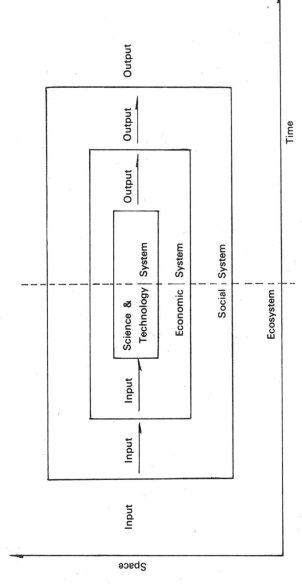

Fig. 2 System Hierarchy in Time and Space Frame

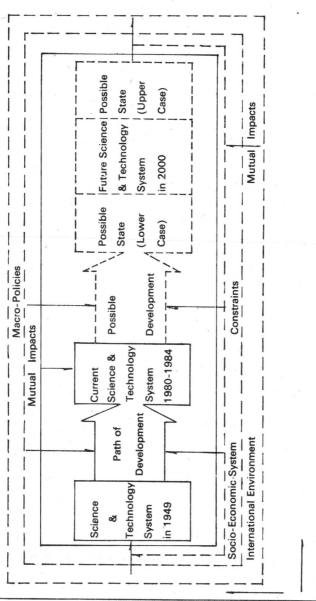

Fig. 3   The Study of Science & Policy in Time and Space Frame

CHAPTER VIII
CHINA'S OPENING TO THE OUTSIDE WORLD

Section 1
Progress Made in Opening to the Outside World

The Third Plenary Session of the Communist Party's 11th Central Committee decided to open China to the outside world. This was a great strategic policy advanced after summing up the historical experience of the country's economic construction over three decades. It was a major turning point which marked the change of China's economy from a closed to an open one. It has produced and will continue to produce a far-reaching impact on the country's development.

Beginning from 1979, China ended the policy of closing itself to external contact and started to face the world. Since then, it has set up special economic zones, open coastal cities, and established a forward belt open to the outside world with a population of more than 200 million and with a gross output value of industry and agriculture accounting for over 50 percent of the national total.

The open policy has promoted the rapid development of China's foreign trade, effectively backed up our economic construction, and expedited changes in our foreign trade patterns. The focus of the policy concerning foreign trade has changed from supplying each other's needs and regulating surplus and deficiencies to making use of the international market and foreign resources to stimulate domestic economic development. We began to make use of our comparative advantages to participate in the international division of labor.

The use of foreign funds has speeded up China's economic construction and the development of various undertakings. We are importing foreign funds from an increasing number of countries, and the methods of using foreign funds have diversified. Since the adoption of the open policy, China has imported huge amounts of equipment and technology, which have helped in our scientific and technological progress and the technological revamp of our enterprises. At the same time, we have conducted extensive academic and technological exchanges and cooperation with other countries, which have improved our scientific and technological level and management level and increased the abilities of some of our products and technologies to participate in international competition.

Opening to the outside world has widened our people's vision immensely and brought about tremendous changes in people's ideas. They have realized the gap between China and the developed countries and begun to accept the ideas of market, competition, and efficiency, which are helpful to our country's modernization. It has strengthened our determination and confidence to build a socialist planned commodity economy. In short, the reform and the open policy ushered in a new era of development in our country.

Section 2
China's Foreign Trade

Since the introduction of the open policy, China's export trade has developed considerably. In 1986, the country's export trade increased more than three times compared with the period before the reform and the proportion of exports as part of the total national income rose from 5.6 percent in 1978 to 12 percent in 1986.

1. China's present foreign trade policy

As a developing socialist country, China has consistently stood for development of trade and economic and technological exchange with all countries of the world on the basis of equality and mutual benefit.

Based on the principle of promoting domestic technological progress, increasing the ability to earn foreign exchange through export, and saving on the use of foreign exchange, we organize in a planned way the import of new technology and key equipment required in national construction, raw materials badly needed in production, and a part of people's daily necessities, but we strictly control the import of non-essential consumer goods. We import advanced, readily usable technologies which have not been mastered at home, with importance attached to the import of software and the prevention of repetitive imports. Our imposts should support the building of the infrastructure such as electricity, transport, raw materials, and energy as well as strategic industries. We should develop import substitutes and raise the proportion of domestically made goods.

At present, 80 percent of our foreign exchange depends on exports. To ensure sustained expansion of exports, we require that the quality of the export products is given top priority so that we can meet the demand of the international market; we have established some bases, factories, and workshops specially producing export products and have gradually established all kinds of export production systems with distinct characteristics; we have made efforts to improve export product mix and carry out the policy of encouraging and fostering the production of export commodities.

What is more important, the reform of the foreign trade system being carried out in China will greatly promote the development of foreign trade. With China's existing price and taxation system and import and export decision-making system, it is difficult to introduce business accounting with overall interest taken into consideration and to achieve the most rational amount and pattern of import and export. The use of economic levers can coordinate the relations between the central government and the enterprises and we should acquire a clear understanding of the best total import and export amount and pattern. Only in this way can the formulation of the economic levers be reliable. To study the optimum trade pattern is of great significance for the formulation of the foreign trade policy.

2. Projection of foreign trade

At present, China stresses the import of advanced technology, key equipment, and materials for production and construction which are in short supply. Taking the export pattern of 1986 as an example, the proportion of manufactured industrial goods increased to 19.1 billion U.S. dollars, accounting for 63.7 percent of total export value. Of this, heavy industrial products accounted for 16 percent; chemical products, 4.3 percent; and light and textile products, 43.2 percent. The export of primary products reached 10.9 billion U.S. dollars, making up 36.3 percent of total exports.

Experts have predicted China's foreign trade on the basis of historical trends in China's level of economic development. From 1981 to 2000, the country's import and export trade will grow at an average annual rate of 8.5 percent, with the growth rate of imports and exports approaching each other.

An analysis of the export pattern shows that the absolute amount of agricultural and food products will increase considerably, but their proportions of total exports will drop visibly; the growth rate of the export of textiles will be higher than that of textile production, the amount of exports will steadily increase, and its proportion of total export products will also rise; the absolute amount of export of ferrous metal products will go up, but its proportion of total exports will drop. This is an indication that among our export products, the proportions of raw materials and primary products are declining. On the other hand, the absolute amount of exports of chemical, machinery, and electronics products will increase, and their proportions of the total exports will also rise. The growth rate of export of chemical products will be similar to that of the industry's production. The growth rate of export of machinery and electronics products will be faster than that of production. The export of petroleum will increase, but its proportion in the export structure. will decrease. Considering that by 2000 China will have a huge accumulation of foreign loans to service and the capital and interest to be repaid will be rather high while the annual inflow of foreign currency will reduce, an increase in the export of manufactured goods is not only the general trend of industrialization but also the demand of industrialization itself.

An analysis of import patterns shows that the proportion of import of ferrous metallurgical products is very high. It will drop somewhat by the year 2000, as that of oil will. The import of chemical products will go up before 1995, and after that it will remain level. The import of machinery and electronics products will rise year by year, and by 2000 it will reach 30-40 percent of total imports. The general trend is that the import of more primary products and basic materials will give way to the import of more advanced technology, equipment, and advanced materials.

The forecast of import and export patterns is based on the possibilities and needs of domestic production. It has to be revised constantly in accordance with various complicated situations and the demands of the international division of labor.

Section 3
China's Import of Foreign Funds

1. The general situation of China's import of foreign funds

Insufficient funds and backward technology are two major factors restraining China's economic development. That's why we regard attracting foreign funds and technology as an important aspect of our opening to the outside world. We actively absorb and make use of foreign loans in all forms and at the same time welcome direct foreign investment and encourage foreign investors to engage in all kinds of production and construction undertakings. By the end of 1986, the loan agreements which China signed with foreign countries, including foreign government loans, loans by international monetary organizations and foreign banks, and bonds issued in foreign countries, totaled 28.9 billion

U.S. dollars, of which 20.56 billion U.S. dollars have been in use. Aside from the capital and interest already repaid, foreign loans totaled 22.84 billion U.S. dollars by the end of June 1987. In conjunction with domestic funds, these foreign funds were mainly used on more than 100 large- and medium-sized construction projects, including large iron and steel complexes, petrochemical enterprises, and more than 20 other large sets of equipment for transport, energy and other key construction projects. Some of these projects have been completed and are now playing a positive role in China's economic development.

China attaches great importance to drawing direct investment from foreign business people. From July 1979, when the Law on Sino-Foreign Joint Ventures was promulgated, to the end of June 1987, a total of 8,513 foreign investment contracts were signed, attracting 21.08 billion U.S. dollars of direct investment by foreign business people, of which 9 billion U.S. dollars have been put in use. In addition, China has cooperated with foreign countries in offshore oil prospecting, and some initial results have been achieved. In a number of contract areas, oil exploitation possesses great possibilities. Investments in commodity credit forms such as leases, financing, and compensation trade have also developed considerably in the past few years. Generally speaking, foreign investors have achieved good economic results from their investments. A small number of foreign-funded enterprises have encountered difficulties of one kind or another in their operations, but with the expansion of China's investment scale and joint efforts of the Chinese and foreign partners, these difficulties can surely be overcome.

2. Continue to improve the investment environment

(a) The fixing of the development strategy of coastal open cities and special economic zones is the main basis for the improvement of the investment environment. The development strategy and planning of China's coastal cities took shape gradually and has placed a corresponding demand on the investment environment. Different strategic proposals have vastly different demands on the infrastructure, direction of investment, and market environment. To make clear the development strategy is itself an important aspect of the investment environment. As the next step, it is necessary to give overall consideration to coordinated arrangements for the development plans of various coastal open cities and to fit them in with the country's overall development. This is of great importance to the improvement of the investment environment.

(b) Infrastructure, science and technology, and social conditions are basic conditions necessary for making investment. Infrastructure facilities are absolutely necessary for the import of foreign funds and advanced technology and for the running of modern factories and service departments. Infrastructure includes the supply of electricity, water, and energy; transport; communication and post and telecommunications; and the guarantee of international communication. All these are essential conditions to attract foreign funds. To create a favorable investment environment in this respect, all coastal open cities have made great efforts to improve their infrastructure. But as a whole the improvement is still inadequate. From a long-range view, it is necessary to set up development zones, but there must be sufficient manpower, material, and financial resources to support the construction of infrastructure facilities in the new zones.

Compared with other parts of the country, the coastal open cities have more scientifically and technologically qualified personnel necessary for the import of foreign technology. However, we must give them adequate training to raise their scientific and technological levels and management expertise still further, especially for specialized personnel.

The import of foreign funds and technology and advanced management knowhow will bring with it different ideas of value. The higher wages of employees of joint ventures will cause new problems of distribution. The quality of the labor force should be raised steadily to adapt to the new wage level and to maintain the superiority of a cheap labor force.

Joint ventures do not exist in isolation but have connections with other enterprises and the whole society. In considering the construction plans of joint ventures, it is necessary to take into account their relations with other supporting industries and their mutual adaptability.

(c) A correct understanding of how best to use foreign funds is an important condition for the continued successful import of foreign funds. Since China's adoption of the open policy, the departments and regions concerned have regularly published progress reports on various projects for Chinese-foreign joint ventures in accordance with the conditions of economic construction and needs. This helped in guiding foreign investment in the right direction, prevented blind investment, and thus increased the economic results of foreign-funded enterprises. With the steady development of the import of foreign funds, these reports published by various regions and departments, could no longer suit the needs. Thus, it was necessary for the state to make an overall plan for the projects using foreign funds according to the needs in all fields and to regularly or as necessary make public disclosures of the progress on these projects and encourage, restrict, or ban foreign investment. Proceeding from the needs of different stages of development of their economies, many countries have made clear their stress on the attraction of foreign funds. China's stress and direction in drawing foreign investments is becoming clear. The Regulations on Encouraging Foreign Investment promulgated by the State Council on October 11, 1986, elucidated this point. However, it is necessary to set forth specific demands on the direction of investment from the angle of the rationalization of the industrial structure.

(d) Strengthening the preliminary work on foreign investment projects, making conscientious feasibility studies, and scientifically making policy decisions on investment projects are important conditions for using foreign funds. Preliminary work is done for most foreign-funded projects but in different ways. For some projects, extensive feasibility studies and work demonstrations were done before the joint venture contract was signed. The investors made correct decisions on the selection of joint venture objective, products, and technology and made realistic forecasts of the joint venture's prospects of operation, market demand for its products, and the reliability of sales of its products in foreign markets. After they went into operation, they achieved good economic results. However, some enterprises did not make market forecasts and did not do thoroughgoing feasibility studies. Some enterprises inappropriately scaled down the amount of investment required in order to secure approval. As a result, they became very passive in fulfilling the project and in some cases failed to continue the projects.

We must persist in making up-to-standard feasibility studies with no exception for foreign-funded projects. In making feasibility studies, we must make thorough investigations and forecasts of the international market demand and trends and ascertain the possibility of exporting the products and achieving a foreign exchange balance. If the products are sold in China, forecasts must be made of domestic market demand and trends. At the same time, forecasts must be made of the prices of domestic and foreign raw materials, energy, and auxiliary materials. The organizations in charge of the examination and approval should conduct evaluations and demonstrations of the projects.

We must give sufficient attention to the question of making scientific decisions on foreign-funded projects. There must be unified regulations concerning the content and depth of the feasibility studies and systematized examination and approval procedures and standards of evaluation to ensure that the projects obtain good economic returns and conform to the need of the country's development.

(e) Tightening control over the use of foreign funds is an important measure to ensure the successful operation of foreign-funded enterprises.

China's economic management system is in the process of reform. The problems that cropped up in the use of foreign funds and management of foreign-funded enterprises over the past few years were the result of defects in the old system. Hereafter, we must give overall consideration to the use of foreign funds and the system of management of foreign-funded enterprises, looking upon it as an important component part of the entire system of economic management. At present, we are urgently in need of an authoritative organization to look after the management of Sino-foreign joint ventures.

Foreign-funded enterprises have their own characteristics in ownership, organizational form, financial management, and economic ties and should enjoy greater decision-making power in the economic management system. The organizational setup, appointment and removal of management personnel, expenditure and management of funds, and organization and arrangement of production of foreign-funded enterprises should be decided by the board of directors and its management agency on condition that they are not in violation of China's laws and regulations. The local governments and various departments concerned should not interfere in their operation and should help them tide over such difficulties as the supply of raw materials and personnel.

Mutual trust and sincere cooperation between the investing parties are the basis of the successful management of a joint venture. The joint venture belongs to both parties and neither side can regard itself as its sole owner. Both parties should have a grasp of the important environment of the enterprise's operations, particularly the links of supply and marketing. Foreign-funded enterprises should without exception keep their account books, which are subject to regular inspection and supervision by administrative organs in charge of them and tax organizations.

(f) A solution to the problem of achieving a balance in foreign exchange earnings and expenditures is an essential condition for the continued development of foreign-funded enterprises. A few foreign-funded enterprises which have gone into operation in China have met the difficulty to balance their foreign exchange earnings and expenditures, which in turn have affected their normal operations. The reason for this state of affairs is that most of the foreign-funded enterprises are geared to the domestic market and only a small number of them cater to the international market. When they made decisions on their projects, they did not have the guidance of an overall planning, and their feasibility studies were not thoroughgoing. In the examination and approval of projects in the future, we should take foreign exchange balance and foreign exchange compensation as key problems for consideration. The proportion of products to be sold in the international market or foreign exchange compensation as clearly defined in the contract should be strictly carried out. Meanwhile, solid market forecast work should be done by these enterprises.

The overall foreign exchange balance of foreign-funded enterprises is based on the foreign exchange earnings of each enterprise. If most of these enterprises have an unfavorable balance of payments, it would be impossible to achieve an overall foreign exchange balance. The Regulations on Encouraging Foreign Investment adopted by the State Council on October 11, 1986, provides for preferential treatment for those productive enterprises whose products are mainly for export and whose foreign exchange has surpluses after deducting from their total annual foreign exchange income the expenditures for production and operation and remittances sent home by foreign investors from their share of profits.

(g) Perfecting legislation and readjusting policies are the key to the steady development of the efforts to attract foreign funds. Since China's adoption of the open policy, the departments concerned have enacted and promulgated a series of important laws and policies, including the Law Governing Sino-Foreign Joint Ventures, and are setting up a legal system. Laws and policies that were promulgated in the past have also been revised in accordance with the new situations arising from our reform of the economic structure and economic development so that they are now more conducive to opening to the outside world and improving the investment environment.

The policies concerning the investment environment are being steadily improved. For instance, preferential policies have been enacted for foreign-funded enterprises which import advanced technology and export products to earn foreign exchange. There are also policies to encourage those enterprises which are conducive to improving the comprehensive returns of the national economy and to improving China's overall industrial structure. In short, policies and legislation should be used to create a sound investment environment and form a force to push ahead the work of attracting foreign funds.

3. Problems calling for attention in understanding China's investment environment.

To have a correct understanding of China's investment environment, it is necessary to examine not only the current but also the growing trends. Since the introduction of the open policy in 1979, our efforts of attracting foreign funds have been mainly confined to the coastal open cities.In the past few years, that is, the period of the Sixth Five-Year Plan, these efforts proceeded without clear direction. Hereafter, we entered a new phase of steady, planned development.

(a) Improving the investment environment is dictated by China's reform and development. Reform and opening to the outside world are China's established policies. Implementation of these policies requires improvement of the investment environment both for domestic funds and foreign capital. China's regulations encouraging foreign investment are in keeping with reform of its investment management system. It can thus be predicted that the country's investment environment will steadily improve.

As the reform of the economic structure advances, China's traditional investment management system, with government investment as the major form, is beginning to change. Various forms of investment have been playing an increasingly important role in building up the country's fixed assets. This provides the basis for considering the reform of the investment management system. We should, in the future, divide the spheres of investment and foster different forms of investment to achieve the fulfillment of our macro-economic targets and to establish an investment management system that coordinates these forms and objectives of investment. In making investments today, enterprises still play a small role because of a lack of financial resources. In the course of the reform, the state and localities should gradually delegate the power of productive investment to enterprises according to the scale of the project and the industries. In this way, investments made by the central authorities, the local governments, and the enterprises can be divided as follows: Investments from central authorities will focus on trans-regional, non-profit making, or little-profit making infrastructure, energy, transport, post and telecommunications, raw materials, and newly emerging industries as well as scientific and technological, educational, and public health undertakings; investments from the local governments will be concentrated on building urban and rural infrastructure facilities, educational and social welfare, and other non- productive undertakings, and the tertiary industries; central and local governments in principle will no longer assume responsibility for investment in general productive enterprises. The decision-making power on productive investments will be gradually handed over to enterprises which will expand production and enhance their competitive capability by relying on their own resources.

This kind of investment system is not only helpful to the building of the infrastructure but also to the shift from direct control to indirect control by the government, a change of profound significance. It will help promote the creation of a commodity market system, including the markets for the means of production, labor service, funds and foreign exchange. The creation and development of the market system is the basic condition for the improvement of the investment environment.

(b) Investing in China is dictated by the development strategy of some countries. The import of foreign capital is important to China's strategic policy of development as well as a component part of the country's overall development strategy. Moreover, investing in China is also required by the development of some countries. The interests of foreign investors reflect the interests of these countries. To improve China's investment environment, primarily that of the coastal open cities, is the concern of both parties. The short-sighted practice of a small number of enterprises which try to make money at the expense of China is harmful to the development of foreign investment in this country. It must be understood that the improvement of China's investment environment is beneficial to the development of this country as well as to that of the other countries concerned.

For example, Japan, through its investments, has stressed expanding its strongholds for export sales and making use of cheap foreign resources and labor. The investments of Japan's manufacturing industries abroad are the largest in the world, and this has resulted in the sharpening of Japan's trade frictions with European countries and the United States. The developing countries have been unsuccessful in trying to achieve a highly effective industrial structure by obtaining advanced technology. Thus, contradictions developed between them and the developed countries. This has made the investment environment more problematic. Improving the investment environment is not only the concern of the recipient country but has much to do with the investor country.

Some people in Japan believe that only when the technological level of China lags behind that of Japan by 15 years can Japan rest assured. In that atmosphere, it would be very difficult for China to obtain required technology from Japan. This is in conflict with China's requirement of importing foreign funds simultaneously with the import of advanced technology. Thus, whether or not the investor country has appropriate policies and principles is also a matter of great importance.

There is a severe trade imbalance between the United States and Japan. The devaluation of the U.S. dollar and revaluation of the Japanese yen has not been of much help in improving this situation. It is rather difficult to try to solve this problem from the angle of the two countries alone. This problem can possibly be better solved by adopting a multilateral strategy. For instance, the United States could actively transfer technologies to China to promote the export of Chinese-made goods to the United States in place of some of the Japanese exports to the United States. The increase of income from trade with the United States would be favorable to China's import of U.S. technology and equipment. This is an illustration of the impact of the strategies of the countries concerned on the improvement of the investment environment.

(c) The import of foreign funds is an important means to accelerate China's economic development. Whether or not foreign funds can be imported successfully hinges on our ability to make use of the imported funds to achieve significant economic returns.

The increase of economic returns, however, depends on the efforts of both the investor and the receiver of the investment.

In the study of "China Towards the Year 2000," experts studied the scale, timing, and manner of China's import of foreign funds and linked them to the country's balance of international payment. They were of the opinion that the import of foreign funds on a large and appropriate scale is in the interest of medium- and short-term economic development, while the amount of the long-range import of foreign funds should be decided by the country's ability to achieve foreign exchange balance though its exports. For this reason, preparations should be made during the Seventh Five-Year Plan and Eighth Five-Year Plan periods for foreign exchange balance during the Ninth Five- Year Plan period and afterwards. The crucial thing is to consider the comprehensive macro-economic returns of foreign funds, to integrate the import of foreign funds and the import of technology, and to enhance the competitive ability of China's export products and its ability to repay capital with interest.

In short, China's investment environment, particularly that of the coastal open cities, will continue to improve. This is not only our country's established policy but is also dictated by the country's reform and development. It is also in keeping with the world trend of development.

Section 4
Some Ideas on the Strategy of Opening to the Outside World

1. Several international economic strategies

In the past three decades or more, the world economy as a whole has experienced rapid and sustained growth and the relative income among nations has never before undergone such conspicuous changes. The most important factor affecting the economic development of various countries after World War II was the success or failure in promoting exports. Some countries which emphasized exports at an early period reaped bountiful rewards. Other countries which paid insufficient attention to exports found it hard to maintain a high growth rate. The World Bank summed up the world's economic strategies into five categories:

(a) A highly open economy without protectionism, such as in Hong Kong; (b) promoting exports, particularly that of manufactured goods, mixed with protectionist measures and measures for government control of the economy, such as in Japan and South Korea; (c) a regional association within which there is free trade of manufactured goods but each country protects its own agricultural production and adopts some protectionist actions towards industrial products from other regions, such as in the European Community; (d) an economy which receives a high degree of protection, has no clear policy direction for exports but has promoted industrialization, and has limited amount of foreign investments, such as in Brazil and India before 1964; and (e) a relatively closed economy which has strict restrictions on trade and investment, such as in China and the Soviet Union before 1979.

Three categories of countries mentioned above actively participate in international trade, but their methods are different, and they produce different effects on their economic growth. There is much room for choice among them.

2. The role and limitations of import substitution

A World Bank report pointed out that some countries once stressed the strategy of import substitution (such as Argentina, Brazil, India, Mexico, and Pakistan). At the beginning, they all went through a period of rapid industrialization, but then they were confronted with diverse problems, including low efficiency, trade deficits, debt crises, inflation, and social instability. These countries have something in common, i.e., they rely on protectionism to stimulate investment in place of imports. This often created a haven for domestic enterprises, allowing them to increase prices to compensate for high production costs without being subject to the pressure of carrying out reform, improving quality, and reducing production costs. As a whole, the system of a national economy constantly demands import of machinery, equipment, and badly needed raw materials, but it is incapable of providing sufficient export products to pay for these needs or to catch up with the technological progress abroad.

Substituting domestic products for imports is actually protecting domestic enterprises. Carrying out industrialization under such conditions will cause domestic prices to be out of step with international prices. The domestic prices of durable consumer goods will rise higher than the prices abroad, while the prices of means of production and primary products will be forced down. This will lead investments astray. To overcome the serious obstacles created by this development strategy, a number of countries have switched to promoting exports.

While analyzing China's trade problems, some foreign specialists said that China seems to be a world unto itself. They opined that to explore such questions as China's domestic trade, its specialized division of labor in various places, and the impact of these factors on China's road to development is like exploring a special kind of international trade and development question. This statement, perhaps going a bit too far, points to the situation in which the country's unified socialist market has not yet been established. Persistence in the import substitution strategy for a long period of time will be detrimental to the formation of a unified market.

3. Selection of China's opening strategy

There are two models of international economic development strategy: the model of import substitute and the model of export oriented. There are three views on choosing our country's strategy. One view is that we should adopt the import substitution strategy. The argument is that China's production level is low and few products are highly competitive for export. On the other hand, there is a huge demand for import and this results in trade deficits. By adopting the import substitution strategy, we can develop the products we need and reduce imports, which is in the interest of balancing the country's foreign exchange earnings and expenditures. The second view is that we should adopt the export-oriented strategy to be supplemented by import substitution. The reason is that since our opening to the outside world, we have basically confined ourselves to the strategy of relying mainly on an import substitution strategy. This is the crucial reason why our economic returns are poor and our international payment still has not got on a sound track. In the light of international experience and our country's conditions, it is imperative to adopt the export-oriented stategy to be supplemented by import substituteion if we are to open the country further to the outside world. The third view is that we should adopt the export-oriented strategy. Only in this way can we enhance the international competitive capacity of our entire national economy and realize the change from attaching importance to speed and quantity to stressing quality and economic returns. This is also favorable to bringing our own advantages into full play and promoting the increase of macro-economic results. International experience shows that Japan and South Korea and some other countries which once adopted the strategy of import substitution ran into difficulties and rapidly switched over to the export-oriented strategy. We should study these international experience carefully and make use of them properly.

Section 5
Problems Concerning the Establishment of Foreign-Funded Enterprises in China

1. Laws and regulations

As early as in 1979, China had published the Law of he People's Republic of China on Chinese-Foreign Equity Joint Ventures, giving permission to foreign companies, enterprises, other economic organizations, or individuals to join with Chinese companies, enterprises, or other economic organizations in establishing joint ventures in China in accordance with the principle of equality and mutual benefit and subject to approval by the Chinese government. In fact, enterprises in service trades make up a large proportion of the joint ventures set up in the past few years. In 1986 the Law of the People's Republic of China on Foreign-Funded Enterprises was promulgated, permitting foreign enterprises, other economic organizations, or individuals to establish solely foreign-funded enterprises in China, and legal provisions were included in the law for the protection of the legal rights and interests of foreign-funded enterprises.

The promulgation of the Interim Provisions for the Use of Land for Construction of Chinese-Foreign Equity Joint Ventures, the Interim Provisions for Preferential Treatment to Overseas Chinese Investment, the Interim Provisions for Preferential Treatment to the Building of Ports and Wharves by Chinese-Foreign Joint Ventures, etc., shows that Chinese laws and regulations concerning the use of foreign funds are being steadily improved.

To improve the investment environment, attract more foreign investment, import advanced technology, raise product quality, increase foreign exchange earnings through export, and develop the national economy, the State Council made public on October 11, 1986 the Provisions on Encouraging Foreign Investment (22 articles) which set forth new provisions on questions concerning foreign investment and preferential treatment measures. The provisions state in particular, "With the exception of those articles clearly stipulated for application to export-oriented enterprises or enterprises with advanced technology, other articles are applicable to all foreign-funded enterprises."

Since October 1986, the Chinese government has successively made public over a dozen detailed regulations concerning the implementation of certain provisions of the document and management measures. The following are a few examples:

(a) The foreign-funded enterprises have the decision-making power to employ people. In accordance with the needs of production and operation, foreign-funded enterprises can fix their organizational setup and the size of their staff. With the help of the labor and personnel department of the locality where they are located, they can recruit workers and other employees by themselves and select competent people for employment through examinations or other forms of assessment. They can dismiss those incompetent people after a period of probation or training as well as the redundant personnel arising from changes in the production and technological conditions of the enterprises. For those workers and staff members who have violated the rules and regulations of the enterprises and caused certain consequences, they can mete out punishment to them on the merit of each case, up to expulsion. This shows that the Chinese government has delegated full authority to foreign-funded enterprises in the employment of people.

The wage level of workers and other employees of foreign-funded enterprises is fixed by the board of directors according to the principle of not lower than 120 percent of the average wages of state enterprises of the same trade and with similar conditions in the district where they are located. This wage level can be adjusted gradually on the basis of economic results of the enterprise. Moreover, apart from paying for the retirement pension, the unemployment fund and housing subsidy, foreign- funded enterprises are exempt from other subsidies to workers and staff. This represents another preferential treatment foreign-funded enterprises enjoy in China.

(b) Chinese organizations can provide guarantee for foreign-funded enterprises. China's monetary institutions which are legally allowed to handle foreign exchange, and non-monetary legal persons with foreign exchange income can provide guarantee for enterprises which have registered in China according to Chinese laws. But they cannot provide a guarantee for the enterprises' registered capital.

(c) The proportion of registered capital of Sino-foreign joint ventures to the total amount of their investment: The registered capital should be compatible with the scale and scope of their production and operation. Various parties to the joint venture share the profits, risks, and losses in proportion to their contributions to the registered capital. According to China's relevant provisions, for joint ventures with a total investment below 3 million U.S. dollars, their registered capital should make up at least 70 percent of the total investment; for those with an investment between 3 million and 10 million U.S. dollars, the proportion should be 50 percent; for those with an investment between 10 million and 30 million U.S. dollars, the proportion should be at least 40 percent.

2. Taxation

To cater to the needs of the economic structural reform and the opening to the outside world, China has made much headway towards perfecting the taxation system and is further improving it. At present, our taxes can be divided into 27 kinds in six categories: (a) Circulation taxes, or regulatory taxes for income in the fields of production and circulation, including product tax, added value tax, business tax, customs duties, agricultural tax, urban maintenance and construction tax; (b) income taxes—these are regulatory taxes on the net income of production managers and individuals, including state enterprise income tax, collective enterprise tax, income tax for urban and rural producers and dealers, individual income tax, and individual income regulatory tax; (c) resources taxes, which are regulatory taxes for the differential incomes of state resources, including the resources tax, land tax, and salt tax; (d) property taxes, which are regulatory taxes levied on property owned by collectives and individuals, including real estate tax, and vehicles and ship use tax; (e) purpose taxes, which are regulatory taxes o special acts and objects, including building tax, bonus tax, wage regulation tax, special fuel consumption tax, livestock transaction tax, slaughtering tax, and fair trade tax; and (f) taxes for dealings with foreigners, which are taxes on handling foreign economic relations, including foreign enterprise income tax, Chinese-foreign equity joint venture tax, individual income tax, and consolidated industrial and commercial tax.

At present, China's circulation taxes account for more than 50 percent of the total tax income and income taxes account for more than 30 percent. When added up, the two kinds of taxes make up about 90 percent of the country's tax income.

The above-mentioned taxes were set up to cover all kinds of economic activities. In fact, productive enterprises in general are levied only a few taxes, namely, product tax, added value tax, business tax, income tax, resources tax, urban maintenance and construction tax, vehicle and ship use tax, and real estate tax.

The state enterprise income tax imposes a fixed rate of 55 percent for large and medium-sized enterprises. Small enterprises and other trades, such as restaurants and catering services, hotels, and hostels are subject to an eight-grade excess progressive tax rate.

3. Taxes for foreign-funded enterprises

(a) Chinese-foreign equity joint venture income tax—The Income Tax Law of the People's Republic of China for Chinese-Foreign Equity Joint Ventures, promulgated in 1980, is aimed to provide legal stipulations for the levy of taxes on Sino-foreign joint ventures in China. According to the law, income tax on the income derived from production, business operations and other sources by branches and sub-branches of a joint venture that are within and outside the territory of China shall be paid by their head office on a consolidated basis.

A 30-percent income tax will be levied on the net income of a Chinese-foreign joint venture (the amount remaining from its gross income after the costs, expenses and losses have been deducted) in a tax year. In addition, a local income tax of 10 percent of the assessed income tax shall be levied. Hence, the total tax rate is 33 percent. In case of a foreign partner remitting out of China its share of profit obtained from the venture, an income tax of 10 percent shall be levied on the remitted amount.

The law includes stipulations on preferential treatment in the levy of income tax for newly established joint ventures, joint ventures in agriculture and forestry which make low profits, joint ventures set up in economically underdeveloped, outlying regions, as well as for those foreign partners who reinvest their share of profits in China.

(b) Income tax for foreign enterprises—The Income Tax Law of the People's Republic of China for Foreign Enterprises was promulgated on December 13, 1981. It provides for tax collection on the income obtained in China by foreign enterprises that have establishments within the territory of China engaged in independent business operations or in cooperative production or cooperative business operations with Chinese enterprises and on foreign economic organizations which have obtained income in China by means of funds, technology, leases, services, and royalties.

The income tax on foreign enterprises is computed at progressive rates on amounts in excess of specified amounts of taxable income as follows: The tax rate for annual income not in excess of 250,000 yuan is 20 percent; for that part of annual income from 250,001 to 500,000 yuan, the rate is 25 percent; for that part of annual income from 500,001 to 750,000 yuan, the rate is 30 percent; for that part of annual income from 750,001 to 1,000,000 yuan, the rate is 35 percent; and for that part of annual income above 1,000,000 yuan, the rate is 40 percent.

When paying the income tax in accordance with the above provisions, the foreign enterprises should also pay a local income tax of 10 percent of the taxable income.

The law also includes preferential tax policy for certain trades and situations.

(c) Individual income tax—The Individual Income Tax Law, promulgated in 1980, is a law governing the levy of taxes on the income of individuals from wages and salaries, remuneration for personal services, royalties, lease of property, and other kinds of income.

There are two kinds of tax rates. First, a progressive rate is levied monthly on wages, salaries, and other regular income which are in excess of necessary living expenses. In other words, an individual income tax is levied on the part of a monthly income in excess of 800 yuan. The rate for that part of total monthly income from 801 yuan to 1,500 yuan is 5 percent; from 1,501 yuan to 3,000 yuan, 10 percent; from 3,001 yuan to 6,000 yuan, 20 percent; from 6,001 yuan to 9,000 yuan, 30 percent; from 9,001 yuan to 12,000 yuan, 40 percent; and from 12,001 yuan upwards, 45 percent.

Second, income from remuneration for personal services, royalties, interest, dividends, extra dividends, and the lease of property and other kinds of income is taxed at a flat rate of 20 percent.

There are also provisions for reduction and exemption from the income tax.

(d) Customs duties—Except for those provided otherwise, all import and export commodities approved by the Chinese government will be levied import tax or export tax in accordance with the Import and Export Tax Regulations of the Customs Office of the People's Republic of China.

China's policy on customs duties is designed to expedite the country's policy of opening to the outside world, to encourage exports, to expand the import of necessities, to protect and promote the development of the national economy, and to ensure the country's customs income. The specific principles in fixing the rates of customs duties are:

(1) Exemptions will be granted to or low rates imposed on the import of fine strains of animals and plants, fertilizer, fodder, medicine, precision instruments, instruments and meters, key machinery and equipment and grain—all of which are necessary to the national construction and the people's livelihood but which cannot be produced domestically or are in short supply;

(2) Low rates will be levied on the parts and accessories of machinery equipment, and instruments and meters which cannot be produced domestically or are produced below standard;

(3) The rates for raw materials are in general lower than semi-finished products or finished products, and low rates will be levied on the import of those raw materials the supply of which cannot meet domestic demand in a short period of time because of restrictions by natural conditions;

(4) Higher import duties are imposed on those commodities which can be produced domestically or which are not essential to the national economy and people's livelihood;

(5) Still higher import duties are levied on those commodities of which the domestic production needs to be protected;

(6) To encourage export, no export duties are levied on most commodities to be exported.

China's import tax rates are divided into ordinary rates and minimum rates. Import commodities from countries which have not signed trade treaties or agreements with China containing articles providing for mutual preferential treatment in customs duties are levied according to ordinary tax rates. Import commodities from countries which have signed these types of agreements will be levied according to the minimum rates.

(e) Consolidated industrial and commercial tax—This tax is imposed on all institutions and individuals for their products or business income. All institutions or individuals who engage in the production of manufactured goods, purchase of agricultural products, import of foreign goods, retail of commodities, and the offering of transport and other types of services are required to pay the consolidated industrial and commercial tax.

The characteristics of the consolidated industrial and commercial tax are that it is levied on the basis of the circulation amount of the industrial and agricultural products and service trades and that it is collected twice in the whole process of production and sale of the commodities, namely, when the manufactured goods are shipped out of the factory and at the time of their retail sale. All foreign and overseas Chinese businessmen engaged in the above-mentioned production and business operations in China may pay the tax according to the consolidated industrial and commercial tax law.

The consolidated industrial and commercial tax is collected according to specific products or business operations. Industrial products are divided into 108 taxable items with 42 tax rates according to different industries and different products and in the light of the principle that the rates for capital goods are lower than that of consumer goods and that of necessities are lower than that of non-necessities. The highest rate, such as for cigarettes, is 69 percent (now reduced to 66 percent), and the next highest is for liquor, at 60 percent. Among the low rates, the rate for machinery products is 5 percent; for gas, 2 percent; and for gray cotton cloth, 1.5 percent. For most commodities, the rates are below 20 percent. There are four rates for commerce, transport services and service trades. The tax rate for transport services is 2.5 percent, for commerce it is 3 percent in general, for hotels and advertisements it is 5 percent, and for consultancy services it is 7 percent.

In the collection of consolidated industrial and commercial

tax, there are also provisions for exemptions and reductions for various forms of Sino-foreign joint ventures.

(f) Real estate tax—The real estate tax introduced in 1951 is a tax imposed on house owners and land users in accordance with the prices of the houses, land, or rent. The tax is levied annually. The rate collected according to the house price is 1.2 percent and that according to rent is 18 percent.

(g) License tax for the use of vehicles and ships—The license tax for the use of vehicles and ships (made public in 1951) is a tax levied on vehicles running on the public roads of the state and on ships sailing in the country's rivers, lakes, or seas based on their varieties and sizes.

The amount of the tax and the areas, date, and methods of collection are worked out by the tax bureaus of the various provinces, autonomous regions, and municipalities directly under the central government.

Both the real estate tax and the license tax for the use of vehicles and ships are local taxes.

(h) To expand economic cooperation and technological exchange with foreign countries and speed up the construction of ports and wharves to meet the needs of China's socialist modernization, the State Council has made special provisions concerning preferential treatment for the construction of harbors and wharves by Sino-foreign joint ventures. The provisions include permission for a longer period of joint operation, reduction of income tax to 15 percent, extension of the period of tax exemption, and allowing the joint ventures to engage concurrently in other projects which require less investment, a shorter construction cycle, and have a higher rate of profit.

(i) Special provisions have been made in relation to the four special economic zones of Shenzhen, Zhuhai, Xiamen and Shantou, and the 14 coastal open port cities of Dalian, Qinhuangdao, Yantai, Qingdao, Lianyungang, Nantong, Shanghai, Ningbo, Wenzhou, Fuzhou, Guangzhou, Zhanjiang, and Beihai. To facilitate the economic cooperation and technological exchange of the special economic zones and coastal cities with other countries, to attract foreign funds, and to import advanced technology to speed up the socialist modernization drive, preferential treatment of exemption or collection at reduced rates of enterprise income tax and consolidated industrial and commercial tax will be accorded to companies, enterprises, and individuals from foreign countries, Hong Kong and Macao who set up Sino-foreign joint ventures, Sino-foreign cooperative enterprises, or solely foreign-owned enterprises in the above-mentioned zones and coastal cities.

China's laws and regulations on taxes concerning Chinese-foreign joint ventures mainly include the Income Tax Law of the People's Republic of China for Chinese-Foreign Equity Joint Ventures, Regulations on the Consolidated Industrial and Commercial Tax of the People's Republic of China (draft), Decree of the Ministry of Finance of the People's Republic of China on Trial Implementation of the Detailed Provisions of the Regulations on the Consolidated Industrial and Commercial Tax of the People's Republic of China, and the Interim Provisions of the State Council of the People's Republic of China for Reduction and Exemption of Enterprise Income Tax and Consolidated Industrial and Commercial Tax in the Special Economic Zones and the 14 Coastal Port Cities. The above-mentioned laws and regulations include provisions on tax collection from service trades.

4. Monetary institutions

China's monetary institutions have developed enormously in the past few years. The central bank system has been established and specialized banks and other banking institutions have been set up. The Agricultural Bank of China is a specialized bank in the field of rural finance, which is in charge of rural credit cooperatives. The Bank of China is an independent bank specialized in dealing with foreign exchange business and also handles credits and loans for foreign trade. The Industrial and Commercial Bank of China handles the deposits, loans, settlements, and loans on technological upgrading of industrial and commercial enterprises as well as savings deposits of urban citizens. The People's Construction Bank of China is mainly in charge of loans for the country's capital construction projects and loans for large technological upgrading projects covered by state plan. Moreover, the China International Trust and Investment Corporation has been set up to handle trust and investment business. The China Investment Bank has also been set up to handle mainly loans from the World Bank. All the specialized banks have branch offices in all parts of the country. Urban credit cooperatives and other financial organizations have been set up in some parts of the country.

The range of credit activities has been expanded and credit funds can now be issued to state enterprises, collective enterprises and individuals. The variety of credit include working funds and fixed asset investments for industrial and commercial enterprises.

Efforts have been made in the past few years to explore flexible and varied forms of credit. A credit management system has been set up, with bank credit as the dominant factor and with commercial credit, non-governmental credit, and other types of credit existing side by side. In line with the macro-economic guidance given by the state and in light of the sources of funds they raise by themselves, the various specialized banks can decide to whom to extend loans and can make inter-bank loans.

To support the production and operation of foreign-funded enterprises and promote China's economic and technological cooperation with other countries, the State Council has approved the Measures of the Bank of China on Extending Loans to Foreign-Funded Enterprises. Loans required by the foreign-funded enterprises are handled by the Bank of China, and this also applies to service establishments opened with foreign investment. The Bank of China handles the following forms of loans to foreign-funded enterprises:

(a) Fixed asset loans used to defray expenses on engineering construction, technology, equipment purchasing, and installation for capital construction projects and technological upgrading projects. The loans are mostly medium- and short-term ones, buyer's loans, banking consortium loans, and project loans.

(b) Working fund loans used as funds required by enterprises in commodity production and circulation and normal business operations. These loans are divided into loans for production, storage and transport, provisional loans, and current deposit overdrafts. (c) Foreign exchange mortgage loans. All Sino-foreign joint ventures, Sino-foreign cooperative enterprises and foreign enterprises, which have registered in China, can apply for renminbi loans by mortgaging the foreign exchange in their possession (including foreign exchange they have brought from abroad). When the terms of the loans expire, they can retrieve their mortgaged foreign exchange after returning the renminbi loans. This will help meet the foreign-funded enterprises' temporary needs for renminbi without having to exchange their foreign exchange into the Chinese currency.

(d) Reserve loans, which are extended on request by an enterprise to be used as reserve funds for a special purpose upon approval by the Bank of China.

In raising a loan from the Bank of China, a joint venture must sign a loan contract with the bank, open a loan account, and go through the formalities outlined in the provisions of the contract.

5. The relevant management organs

The following management organs are concerned with foreign investment:

(a) The State Planning Commission is a comprehensive planning institution of the state in charge of examining and approving the projections and feasibility studies of Chinese-foreign joint ventures which require investments above certain amounts. The maximum limits for different places are different. For instance, for Shanghai, the limit is 30 million U.S. dollars; for Guangdong, 10 million U.S. dollars; Beijing, 10 million U.S. dollars; and other provinces and municipalities, 5 million U.S. dollars.

(b) The Ministry of Finance participates in examining foreign-invested projects; helps drawing up accounting statutes, rules, and regulations for Chinese-foreign joint ventures and cooperative enterprises; and formulates plans for financial legislation and organizes the drafting of major financial laws and regulations. The State General Taxation Bureau under the ministry is in charge of international negotiations involving taxation on foreign enterprises and the drawing up of agreements and draft agreements.

(c) The Auditing Administration is a state organ exercising auditing supervision over financial and economic activities. It conducts auditing supervision over the financial revenue and expenditures of various departments under the State Council and local governments at all levels and the financial income and expenditure of state financial and monetary organizations and enterprises and institutions.

(d) The Ministry of Foreign Economic Relations and Trade manages and coordinates the foreign trade of various provinces, autonomous regions, municipalities directly under the central government, and the relevant departments of the State Council. It is responsible for the use of foreign funds, organizing import and export of technology, helping in contracting foreign engineering and labor service projects, and promoting multilateral and bilateral economic and technological cooperation among nations. It is also in charge of the General Administration of Customs on behalf of the State Council, gives guidance to the work of the China Council for the Promotion of International Trade, manages inspection of import and export commodities, administers economic and trade organizations and enterprises abroad, and examines and approves the setting up of representative offices for foreign companies in China.

(e) The Ministry of Labor and Personnel is a comprehensive department in charge of the labor and personnel work of the whole country. It is responsible for the country's labor wages, labor employment, labor insurance, labor welfare, and the size of government departments. It controls the labor wages of Chinese-foreign joint ventures and cooperative enterprises.

(f) The Ministry of Materials and Equipment (formerly the State Bureau of Materials and Equipment) maps out the balanced distribution plan for major materials and equipment under unified state control according to the requirement of the State Planning Commission and organizes and directs the placing of orders and dispatch, supply, and control of important materials and equipment. It also organizes and directs the cooperation of various regions and departments in materials and equipment supply.

(g) The State Administration of Commodity Prices is an organization controlling the pricing work of the whole country. It is in charge of the unified management and overall balance of the commodity prices of the whole country and fixes and adjusts the prices of important industrial and agricultural products, prices for communication and transport, standard charges for services, price for import and export commodities, and charges for tourist services involving foreigners. It also establishes the principles and methods for the purchase of materials and the marketing of products by foreign-funded enterprises.

(h) The State Administration for Industry and Commerce is responsible for carrying out economic supervision over industrial and commercial enterprises and market trade, protecting legal operation, banning illegal operation, safeguarding social economic order, promoting production, and invigorating circulation. It handles the registration of domestic industrial and commercial enterprises, Chinese-foreign joint ventures and cooperative enterprises, enterprises run by businessmen from Hong Kong and Macao, and solely foreign-funded enterprises and resident representative offices of foreign companies, and their registration for permanent residence as economic entities and exercise control and supervision over them.

(i) The General Administration of Customs is a state organization supervising and controlling imports and exports. Through its supervision and control of commodities, means of transportation, postal matters and luggage and articles of passengers entering and leaving Chinese territory, collection of customs duties, and banning of smuggling, it safeguards the effective enforcement of the government's principles, policies, and regulations concerning import and export in defense of the country's sovereignty and interests.

To meet the needs of the open policy and facilitate foreign economic relations and trade and international exchange and the supervision and control by the customs offices, customs organizations have been set up at open coastal ports and places where import and export are concentrated. There are 135 customs offices in the country, spreading over 25 provinces, autonomous regions, and municipalities directly under the central government, with the exception of Qinghai, Ningxia, and Gansu. The General Administration of Customs has set up a branch in Guangzhou to strengthen leadership over the customs offices in Guangdong Province.

The formalities for the reduction, exemption, and approval of customs duties are handled by the General Administration of Customs, and the specific business is handled by local customs offices.

CHAPTER IX
CHINA TOWARDS
THE YEAR 2000

In our study, we departed from the traditional model used in the past and adopted a new approach. Starting with the population forecast and the goal to achieve a fairly comfortable standard of living for the people, we examined the economic, scientific, technological, and social factors of development, and on this basis we painted a picture of what China might look like in the future.

Through concrete analysis and study we can see that China's future is bright, but the road ahead is beset with difficulties. To attain the projected goal, we must map out an overall strategy of economic, scientific, technological, and social development under the guiding principle of exploring a road of socialist modernization with Chinese characteristics.

Section 1
China's National Conditions

1. China in the primary stage of socialism

A correct understanding of the historical stage our society is in at present is a matter of primary importance for the building of socialism with Chinese characteristics and is the basis for our formulation and implementation of a correct line and policy. On this question, the Chinese Communist Party has made a clear and definite statement: China is now in the primary stage of socialism.

There are two aspects to this thesis. First, Chinese society is already a socialist society, and we must persevere in socialism and never deviate from it. Second, China's socialist society is still in its primary stage. We must proceed from this reality and must not jump over this stage.

China used to be a semi-colonial, semi-feudal country. Experience since the middle of the nineteenth century shows that the capitalist road is a blind alley for China and that the only way out is to take the socialist road. However, as our socialism was born out of a semi-colonial and semi-feudal society with our productive forces lagging far behind those of the developed capitalist countries, we are destined to go through a very long primary state to achieve industrialization and the commercialization, socialization, and modernization of production which many other countries had achieved under capitalist conditions.

After more than 30 years of socialist development, China has scored successes that have attracted worldwide attention. The economic strength of our country has grown enormously, and our educational, scientific, and cultural undertakings have expanded considerably. On the other hand, our country has a huge population and a poor foundation to start with, and our average per-capita GNP still ranks among the lowest in the world. As the report to the 13th Party Congress has pointed out, "The picture is very clear: Out of a population of more than one billion, 800 million people live in rural areas and, for the most part, still use hand tools to make a living. A certain number of modern industries coexist with many industries that are several decades or even a century behind present-day standards. Some areas that are fairly developed economically coexist with vast areas that are underdeveloped and impoverished. A small amount of science and technology is up to the highest world standards, while the scientific and technological level as a whole is low, and nearly one-quarter of the population is still illiterate or semi- literate." This situation reminds us that a sober understanding of the basic national conditions and the historical stage of our socialist society is a matter of utmost importance.

The primary stage of socialism in China is not the initial phase in a general sense, a phase that every country goes through in the process of building socialism; it is the specific stage China must necessarily go through while building socialism under conditions of backward productive forces and an underdeveloped commodity economy. It is a stage during which we must rid ourselves of poverty and backwardness and achieve a highly developed commodity economy.

2. Re-understanding China's historical stage of socialism

That China is in the primary stage of socialism is a new understanding of our national conditions and the present phase of development. After more than 30 years of building our socialism, a socialist economic system based on public ownership of the means of production has been instituted, a socialist political system of the people's democratic dictatorship has been established, and the guiding role of Marxism in the realm of ideology has been ensured. However, our productive forces are still very backward, which shows that there are still many imperfect aspects to the relationship between production and the superstructure. That's why we are in the primary stage of socialism. It is necessary to have a new understanding of this state of affairs, as we failed to do so in the past.

In fact, this lack of understanding is not confined only to our country. Many other socialist countries have similar problems. In the Soviet Union, Stalin formally announced in 1936 that "The Soviet society has basically realized socialism and established the socialist system." Khrushchev stated in 1961 that the Soviet Union "has entered into the new period of historic development from socialism to communism" and declared that it would basically accomplish the building of a communist society by 1980. Modifying Khrushchev's statement, Brezhnev declared in 1967 that the Soviet Union had built a developed socialism. Later, Andropov asserted that the Soviet Union was "at the starting point of the long historic stage of developed socialism." Now Gorbachev is trying to prove that the Soviet Union is still in the stage of developing socialism.

There are also some inappropriate viewpoints in China in the past. In the autumn of 1958, the Beidaihe Meeting of the CPC Central Committee announced that after seven or eight years, the principle of distribution according to needs could be carried out. The Wuchang Meeting held at the end of the same year corrected this view, pointing out that we were still in the primary stage of socialism, and this stage was a long one. During the "cultural revolution," Chairman Mao stated that distribution according to work and money were both bourgeois right. Since the Third Plenary Session of the 11th Party Central Committee held in December 1978, we have changed that view and set forth the thesis that we are in the primary stage of socialism. This was made clear in the Resolution on Certain Questions in the History of Our Party Since the Founding of the People's Republic of China adopted by the Sixth Plenary Session of the 11th Party Central Committee in 1981. This was again mentioned in the report to the 12th Party Congress and was further confirmed in the Resolution of the Communist Party Central Committee on Guiding Principles for Building Socialist Society With Advanced Culture and Ideology adopted in 1986. The 13th Party Congress made an overall analysis of the primary stage of socialism which marked a new development in Marxist theory. The congress made clear that the primary stage is a considerably long historic period and that it will take about 100 yeas from now to complete this phase.

3. China's basic national conditions

we have a vast territory, but our economic development is highly unbalanced; we have large population and rich resources of manpower, but our educational and technological levels are low, which burdens our society and economy and brings difficulties; our economic construction and educational development have been in considerable scale, but our level of economic development is rather low, our science and technology are backward, and, in particular, our infrastructure facilities are inadequate, our energy supply is strained, and we are short of funds. We have established an advanced socialist political system and economic system but need to improve them. The defects of our economic system formed over the years still have formidable inertia and require drastic reform. Our opening to the outside world has enabled us to draw on the experience of other countries and make use of foreign funds, technology, and markets, but we are subject to capitalist restrictions and obstructions and the corrosion of decadent ideas. The hardships of the ten-year turmoil of the "cultural revolution" have brought to our nation a new awakening, the Party's leadership has improved and further matured, and the Chinese people who are resolved to institute reforms are exploring a socialist road with Chinese characteristics.

A correct understanding and unwavering economic goals are the basis for our formulation of various policies. The recognition of economic relations and the role of economic levers and mastery of the economic levers form the basis of policy making. Close coordination between various policies can ensure the success of the reform, which will improve the conditions for economic development and enable us to set new targets. Accordingly, our study starts with an understanding of our national conditions and an analysis of the favorable and constraining factors. Then we fixed our targets in an effort to bring our advantages into full play and to overcome our disadvantages. To attain our targets, we mapped out policies which could give full scope to our national strength and bring about the self-sustained growth of our national economy. In this way, we can reinforce our national strength and provide reliable guarantees for the fulfillment of our targets. By so doing, it is possible for us to free ourselves from the old model which had hampered the growth of our national economy over a long time, draw on the useful experience of the development strategies of the developed and developing countries, and decide on an effective development strategy which conforms to our national conditions.

Section 2
Development and Economic Growth

1. Coordinated economic, scientific, technological, and social development

The development of human society, which is usually called as coordinated development of economic, scientific, technological, and social factors, is determined by the inherent interdependence, mutual promotion, and contradictions among these factors.

There are different interpretations of the concept "development," and there are different understandings of the meaning of national development. Even in the same country, the understanding of the concept in different periods may not be the same. The development we speak of refers to comprehensive development.

(a) Scientific and technological development: Science and technology is the general term for the knowledge, skills, experience, and theories created and mastered by mankind in scientific experiments and the practice of production to recognize and reform nature. Scientific development includes scientific inventions as well as technological revolution and technological innovation. Technological innovation is the progressive changes in technology, while technological revolution is a historic, qualitative breakthrough and leap forward in the development of technology. Progressive changes in technology occur constantly, while technological revolution takes place only after a long cycle. Scientific and technological development can also be construed as modernization of productive forces which find expression in man's increasing ability to conquer nature. Scientific revolution is a harbinger of technological revolution, while technological development is a bridge between scientific development and the growth of production. Only through a technological revolution can scientific revolution be turned into actual productive forces.

(b) Economic development: Economic development refers to the increase of production, the enhancement of economic strength, the development of social wealth, and the rise in the level of economic growth.

(c) Social development: Society in its broad sense often refers to the modern society of mankind. From this perspective, economy, science, and technology are embraced in society. In exploring the relations between economy, science, and technology and society, society refers to all things outside of economy, science, and technology. Naturally, it includes the environment. Another view is that social development mainly refers to the improvement of people's social lives including material life, spiritual life, political life, and natural environment.

Close relations exist between economy, science, and technology and the society, and this interaction has a positive and a negative side. The interaction is first of all a relation of mutual promotion, and it is precisely this that has pushed ahead human progress. This is particularly true of the progress of mankind in modern times. For instance, economic growth provides a material basis for social development. Rising productivity creates conditions for people to divert manpower and material resources to scientific research and improve the technology of production which in turn stimulates the faster growth of production. However, contradictions also exist between them. For example, excessively fast growth of production will impose tremendous burdens on the economy and bring with it a series of social problems. Rash economic advance will bring about destruction of production and social instability. Scientific and technological progress can create well-being for mankind and can also cause disasters. We must promote the positive relations between economy, science, and technology and the society and reduce the contradictions in among them to the minimum or, if possible, eliminate them completely. This is a problem we have to take into account and solve in studying the development strategy.

2. Development and growth

There are all kinds of standards for development. From the point of view of science, technology, and economy, the countries in the world can be divided according to the people's average per-capita income and the level of scientific and technological development. Judging by these standards, there are also vast differences in the development of all countries.

After World War II, countries in the world chose different roads of development and achieved different advances. They were faced with all kinds of problems, many of which were of worldwide importance. In the three decades between 1950 and 1980, the world economy as a whole experienced rapid and protracted growth heretofore unknown. The relative income of various countries had never before gone through such conspicuous changes.

It is a difficult task to analyze such a complicated problem as the development of mankind. Moreover, the problem of giving too much attention to economic growth which occurred in our country has now become a thing of the past. But domestic and foreign experiences of the present and the past have all demonstrated that what we are after should be overall development instead of economic growth only. Development refers to stable, sustained development and coordinated development, and the former is conditioned by the latter. In this sense, coordinated development is the foundation of development.

There are many special treatises on how to differentiate overall development from economic growth. But we have to put forward our own view through our study because China has to take its own road of development. How to evaluate the achievements of development is itself a complicated question. Its meaning is different in different countries and different societies. Even in one country, there are different standards of achievement in different periods. Take China for example. The standards for evaluating development achievements today differ from those before the Third Plenary Session of the 11th Party Central Committee. In short, economic growth refers to simply pursuing the growth rate of GNP or the gross output value of industry and agriculture, while development has at least the following implications: stable and sustained economic growth; increase of average per-capita GNP; universal benefits received by the people as a result of the economic growth, which promote common prosperity; increased ability to promote technological progress and catch up with the trend of world scientific and technological progress; a higher degree of the country's independence under the conditions of opening to the outside world; constant adjustment of the economic structure and regional structures to meet the needs of development; and, avoidance of the sharp social conflicts that have been severely detrimental to many developing countries. In fact, this illustrates from another angle that only coordinated social, economic, scientific, and technological development is real development and that simple economic growth is not. By affirming coordinated development, we are in essence negating the strategy of solely pursuing economic growth.

Section 3
Some Thoughts on Coordinated Development

1. On the subject of coordinated economic, scientific, technological and social development

Some people hold the view that the correct phrasing should be "coordinated social, economic, scientific, and technological development." Putting the word "social" ahead of the rest stresses the role of the non-economic factor in economic development. Socialism should attach importance to the study of society. The development of mankind, in the final analysis, refers to the development of human society. In the study of the development strategy in the past, most people gave first place to economy. Stressing social development is an attempt to promote the growth of the productive forces from the angle of society, science and technology. It does not contradict with the view of focusing on economy. To attach importance to the study of the capacity of social endurance in the reform will give great impetus to the integration of development and reform at present.

Another view is that the phrasing should be "coordinated economic, scientific and technological, and social development," putting economy at the core of the matter. This is in keeping with the formulation and the essence of the report to the 13th Party Congress. The conclusion drawn and the proposals made on this basis conform to the thinking of the leadership and can thus more easily play their role in the ongoing development and reform.

The third view maintains that the phrasing of "coordinated scientific and technological, economic, and social development" would be more appropriate. This is because in the report to the 13th Party Congress, the first major task in the section on the strategy for economic development is "to give first priority to the expansion of scientific, technological, and educational undertakings, so as to push forward economic development through advances in science and technology and improved quality of the work force." Poor economic results are attributable to the lack of attention to science and technology. To give priority to science and technology stresses their influence on economic and social development. We are of the opinion that to study the relations of coordinated development of the economy, science and technology, and society from different angles is necessary for the exploration of this question.

2. Strategy, model, and mechanism

One view holds that since the question of coordinated social, economic, and scientific and technological development is a strategic question and is the new starting point of our country's development strategy, we should study and articulate them carefully. In this way we can have a systematic, all-round study. Strategy includes objectives, policies, channels, models or mechanisms.

Another view maintains that we should study mechanisms because they are important in coordinating our efforts, and reform is designed to establish a new mechanism of economic operation. At the same time, it should be a coordinated social, economic, scientific, and technological mechanism, otherwise it cannot be carried out. Thus mechanism is more important than model and is the core of the strategy.

Model should integrate with exploring the road of socialist modernization with Chinese characteristics. We should stress the model with Chinese characteristics and stress the principles and standards used to conform coordinated development. After exploring the formation of the mechanism of coordinated development, we should select the core of strategic study. In this way, our present general objective and basic line will be closely integrated.

3. Objectives and targets

It is a consensus of opinion that objective is a collective

concept, that is, a systematic concept. Target is used to measure how far the objective has been accomplished. The designing of the objective system and the fixing of targets are contents of the strategic study as well as the standards that have to be set in actual work. However, we must have a clear definition of the general objective of coordinated development. The following are a few definitions.

"For coordinated development, it is necessary to develop productive forces and center on developing productive forces."

"It is necessary to make the objective of socialist production of meeting the people's ever growing material and cultural needs the objective and standard."

"Coordinated development should be aimed at achieving the civilization, prosperity and progress of society, and the people's rising standard of living."

"The objective of coordination should be the all-round development of man."

"Coordinated development should be subordinated to and serve the general objective and the general requirement of the 11th Party Congress."

Do these definitions agree with each other or are they contradictory? Our initial analysis shows that they can agree with each other if they are interpreted in the following context.

First of all, our objective must be subordinated to the guideline, which is of far-reaching significance, set forth at the 13th Party Congress, i.e., "The fundamental task of a socialist society is to expand the productive forces. During this primary stage (of socialism) we must shake off poverty and backwardness, and it is therefore especially necessary for us to put the expansion of the productive forces at the center of all our work. Helping to expand the productive forces should become the point of departure in our consideration of all problems, and the basic criterion for judging all our work should be whether it serves that end." In studying coordinated development, we are aiming to promote faster and more appropriate development of the productive forces.

This requirement completely tallies with the objective of

socialist production, namely, to constantly satisfy the people's growing material and cultural needs, because this can be achieved only by expanding the productive forces. The report delivered at the 11th Party Congress also pointed out, "With the growth of production, we have started to solve, or found ways for solving, certain serious social and economic problems which had long plagued us."

The civilization and prosperity of society should concur with the demand for building an advanced culture and ideology. The formulation which states "coordinated development should be aimed at the civilization, prosperity and progress of society and the people's rising standard of living" should be stressed after the people have attained a fairly comfortable standard of living. During the period of striving for such a life, the material foundation is more important.

As to the definition that the objective coordinated development should be the all-round development of man, we should study the problem by analyzing the relations between the requirements of the 13th Party Congress and the medium-and long-term objectives. This will help realize the requirements of the 13th Party Congress. The first major task defined in the section on the strategy for economic development in the report to the congress is, "To give first priority to the expansion of scientific, technological, and educational undertakings, so as to push forward economic development through advances in science and technology and improved quality of the work force." At present, the all-round development of man should stress the improvement of the quality of individuals.

All these definitions can be unified with the short-term, medium-term, and long-term objectives or the development of the objective at various stages.

4. Mechanism of coordination and mechanism of competition

The mechanism of socialist planned commodity economy should be a system of inherent unity of the planning and the market. The scope of the role of planning and market covers the whole society. The new mechanism of economic operation as a whole should be a system under which "the state regulates the market and the market guides enterprises." Some people think that the mechanism of the market guiding enterprises in essence means the mechanism of competition, that the mechanism of coordination should be subordinated to the mechanism of competition, and the former should help promote the creation of the latter. Some people believe that the mechanism of coordination is a development mechanism, and the mechanism of competition is a reform mechanism. The combination of the two is a "mechanism under which the state regulates the market and the market guides the enterprises." Some other people think that since development is the objective and reform the means, then the coordination mechanism is the objective to be achieved through market competition. Still others declare that "the socialist economic management system is a system integrating competition with intervention," and the planned commodity economy lies in the government giving guidance to the market. They pointed out that the market is oriented towards the formation of the coordination mechanism through competition and intervention. Our view is that the coordination mechanism is to be shaped through the competition mechanism, and the two coincide with each other. But competition should also be under guidance. Otherwise, competition can lead to a course opposite to coordinated development.

5. Coordinated development and the reform

China's economic structural reform has achieved momentous successes and injected new vitality into socialism. All the reforms we have carried out are in the interest of the growth of the socialist economy. In addition, to carry out reform in such a large country like China is itself a process of learning. Our study of coordinated development is aimed at promoting faster and more effective development of the productive forces, which is identical with the objective of the reform. Moreover, coordinated development will help increase the ability of the society to go through the reform, while reform will stimulate coordinated development. In other words, in studying coordinated development we are mainly studying the coordination between development and reform.

6. Coordinated development and opening to the outside world

Coordinated development and opening to the outside world are consistent with each other. The two are inter-linked and promote and condition each other. The opening is an outcome of social, economic, scientific, and technological development to a certain stage and is the basic condition for coordinated development of the country and various regions. It is an essential condition for the integration of the world economy. It means that countries of different systems seek common ground while retaining their differences; they understand, unite, and coordinate with one another. No country's economy which is divorced from the world economy can exist and develop. Meanwhile, coordination pushes ahead opening to the outside world in the movement of contradiction.

7. National coordination and regional coordination

National coordination is based on regional coordination. There can be unified standards and requirements for regional coordination, but there is no unified model. It is precisely because that the regional coordination can give better expression to the comparative advantages of various places and a national coordination can take shape. As to whether there are contradictions between regional coordination and national coordination, this involves the coordination between national interests and local interests. This problem can be solved by taking into account the national interests and the local interests or the rational distribution of both interests, and this is a problem that should be solved through the reform.

As to the question of whether or not localities refer to the present administrative areas or provinces and municipalities, one view holds that economic development zones are not entirely the same as administrative areas, but for the convenience of macro-economic management, administrative areas will serve the purpose. As coordinated development is a high-level problem, it is improper to have too many levels. Generally, it should be divided into three levels: the state, provinces or municipalities, and medium-sized cities or districts.

8. Coordinated development, fairness and efficiency

Some economists at home and abroad maintain that fairness and efficiency are contradictory, that socialist countries excel in fairness but are not as efficient as the capitalist countries with market economies. However, the reform of the socialist countries is in a sense aimed at developing the productive forces effectively to match in efficiency the capitalist countries with market economies. Coordinated development helps promote the improvement of overall efficiency, but economic and social coordination in a certain sense embodies coordination of efficiency and fairness. Fairness is not egalitarianism. Gaps in income to a certain extent are favorable to the development of the commodity economy. But there must be measures to promote common prosperity. This is coordination required from other angle.

9. Coordinated development and balanced development

Balanced relations in a given period are mainly the concept of a static state, while coordination is invariably in a dynamic state. Balance stresses the relations of mutual restraint, while coordination lays emphasis on promotion.

Balance refers to the mutual relations in quantity, while coordination is an analysis of the whole including both quantity and quality. Balance is mainly used to analyze things of the past, while coordinated relations can be used to analyze the present and to explore for the future. Coordination has to be based on a certain amount of balance, or to put it another way, coordination is a dynamic state of balance.

10. Present coordination and future coordination

Coordination has immediate, medium-term, and long-term objectives, and the advance towards the objectives of coordinated development is a gradual process. If the requirements of present coordination are consistent with those of future coordination, then the present coordination is the basis of future coordination, and the coordination mechanism set up will help in the realization of future coordination. If the requirements of future coordination are not the continuation of the development of the requirements of the present coordination, there will appear the inconsistency of the objectives of coordination. In other words, when the present coordination switches to the future coordination, there will be a period of adjustment or the appearance of discoordination. Therefore, in studying coordinated development, we have to sum up the past, base ourselves on the present, and look ahead to the future.

Section 4
China's Overall Development Strategy

1. Choose a sustained, stable, and coordinated development strategy

In the primary stage of socialism, the historical task to be tackled in developing the social productive forces is to strive for industrialization, and to commercialize, socialize, and modernize production. According to the strategic plan for China's economic construction, our GNP will double and the people will lead a fairly comfortable life by the end of this century. Our development strategy has to be fixed on the basis of this requirement. At the same time, we must make preparations to fulfill the task of increasing the average per-capita GNP to the level of moderately developed countries and basically realize modernization by the middle of the twenty-first century.

Based on the understanding of our objectives and national conditions and through forecast and comparison, we have discarded the heavy structure scheme and super high-speed development scheme and chosen the scheme of sustained, stable, and coordinated development of the national economy. The gist of the scheme is to coordinate organically the growth rate, the economic returns, and the people's material benefits. The main points are as follows. Our forecast and analysis are based on consumption, because the purpose of production in socialist society is to satisfy the people's ever increasing material and cultural needs to the maximum. This is the point of departure in the study of the development strategy and policy as well as its end result. The study shows that there are different consumption patterns for the appropriate consumption level to be selected. The conditions in essential factors of production and resources determine a set of appropriate consumption patterns and industrial structure. We can take these consumption patterns as a long-range objective and make the maximum use of various essential factors of production to promote the modernization of the industrial structure and thereby achieve a still higher level of consumption and enable the people to gain more material benefits.

2. Strictly control population growth

To ensure the realization of a fairly comfortable standard of living for the people, it is necessary to strictly carry out the policy of family planning. As one of our national policies, this policy has achieved remarkable results in the past few years. We should continue to make strenuous efforts to implement the policy in the future and try by every possible means to limit the population to 1.25 billion by the end of this century. Now, the newly increased population of our country every year amounts to the entire population of Australia. From 1981 to 2000, our planned net increase of population is more than 200 million, almost equivalent to the present population of the United States or twice the population of Japan. To achieve a fairly comfortable standard of living for our one billion people plus the increased population is a herculean task for any country, even developed countries, such as the United States and Japan.

We should adopt the policy of combining government arrangement for employment with the laborers seeking jobs themselves and set up a flexible employment system integrating urban with rural areas. In this way, we can create jobs for a colossal number of 250 million people in 15 years.

3. Fix an appropriate consumption pattern

The trend in the development of our country's consumption pattern is that the proportion of consumption on agricultural products declines relatively while consumption on housing gradually goes up. In the course of the changes of the consumption pattern, more consumption on housing, better clothing, increased durable consumer goods, development of social services, and higher quality of food will replace the present excessively high proportion for consumption on food. At present, our food grain production allows us to be basically self-sufficient, and the people's nutrition is basically ensured. As our country's per- capita average share of cultivated land is rather small, the production of fodder and the development of livestock raising are restricted. Thus in our food production, we should not seek to achieve the standards of the developed countries, unduly stressing the high proportion of animal foods, because such a diet has become a lesson to draw in the developed countries. As many people in these countries have been plagued by obesity, they have begun to seek healthy food and reduce the proportion of animal fat in their diet. In accordance with our traditional diet and modern nutriology, we should avoid the high-calorie and high-fat food patterns. The calories from animal food should increase from 7.7 percent in the total calories of food intake in 1980 to about 12 percent in 2000. This seems to be an appropriate figure. Otherwise, grain production will not be able to meet the need for livestock raising.

We advocate appropriate consumption, namely, that the consumption level and consumption pattern should be compatible with our country's economic development and our ability of supply. Hereafter, we should encourage people to change their consumption pattern in the direction of commercialized housing, durable consumer goods, and the socialization of household labor.

4. Promote modernization of the industrial structure

After the consumption pattern is fixed, it must be supported by a corresponding industrial structure. The trend of change in our country's industrial structure is that while all industries expand generally, the proportions of agriculture and primary energy decline relatively, and the proportions of transport, post and telecommunications, building materials, machine-building, electronics, and particularly service trades will go up. This is in line with the trend of development of the industrial structure in other countries.

We should persevere in attaching utmost importance to the strategic position of agriculture, promote an overall development of the rural economy, and adjust the structure of agriculture. Under the guidance of the policy of combining trade with industry and agriculture, we should step up the production of commodity grain and accelerate commodity circulation in the rural areas. We should advance from developing crop production alone to developing a "big" agriculture and promoting the all-round development of agriculture, forestry, animal husbandry, sideline occupations, and fishery as well as the comprehensive development of agriculture, industry, trade, and transport.

While making energetic efforts to develop the consumer good industry, we should give ample attention to basic industries and infrastructure facilities. We should speed up the growth of the energy industry while centering on electricity and foster growth of the raw materials industry as well as the iron and steel, nonferrous metals, chemical raw materials, and transport and communications services,thus creating a comprehensive transport system and information dissemination system as the backbone of the industrial structure. We should strive to invigorate machine-building and electronics industries in order to provide increasing quantities of advanced technological equipment and accelerate the growth of newly rising industries with microelectronics, optical fiber communication, and new materials industries in the lead. We should give priority to supporting the manufacturing industries which have competitive abilities for export. We should give adequate attention to transport, communications, and power industries which restrict the development of the national economy to lay the groundwork for economic take-off in the late 1990s.

While promoting coordinated growth of the primary and secondary industries, we should attach importance to the development of tertiary industries. We should pay particular attention to the development of education, information, consultancy, finance, social security, and social service trades and open more channels for employment. We should give priority to promoting the modernization of production and social life, raising economic effects, and increasing the GNP. We should adjust the industrial structure to promote its modernization.

5. Select the technological structure to meet the challenge

In our economic construction, we shoulder the dual task of pushing ahead the traditional industrial revolution and catching up with the new technological revolution in the world. To fulfill this task, it is necessary to go through a long period of hard work systematically and stage by stage. Moreover, it is necessary to combine the two tasks. Against this background, we should adopt new technologies, transform traditional technologies, renovate the equipment, train the technological work force, and raise our technological level in a planned way in order to improve product quality, reduce material and labor consumption, realize rational distribution of the essential factors of production, increase the efficiency of our use of funds, and maximize the resources utilization rate.

We should fix the technological structure with a view to meeting the challenge. In scientific research and the import of technology, we should pay equal attention to traditional technology and high technology. For a considerable period to come, we should devote our main efforts to developing traditional technology. In the development of high technology, we should give pride of place to electronic information technology and attach prime importance to the transformation of traditional industries and traditional technologies. We should improve traditional technologies by creating a large number of "technological compounds" which integrate high technology with traditional technology. In adopting this strategy, we should see to it that high-tech factors permeate into the development of all traditional technologies.

6. Select a strategy that gives priority to science and technology

According to the report to the 13th Party Congress, "Modern

science and technology and modern management are the decisive factors in improving economic results and the principal means of enabling the economy to advance to a new stage of growth. We must recognize clearly that we will get nowhere if we try to develop the economy on the basis of backward technology and management and by consuming enormous resources."

Science and technology are huge productive forces. China has low average per-capita resources, a strained energy supply, backward transport, and insufficient funds. The best way to overcome these restrictions is to elevate the scientific and technological level to obtain more raw materials, energy, and funds. However, a lot of resources have been wasted. Some studies report that at least two-thirds of the material resources we have wasted can be used again without marked change in our lifestyle. Through the design of durable and easily recoverable products, industrial waste materials can be greatly reduced. This plus the implementation of a wise capital goods supply policy will make it possible to raise the resources utilization rate enormously. To this end, it is necessary to rely on science and technology to make rational use of existing materials, create new materials, turn wastes into useful materials, and make comprehensive use of available materials to ease the shortage of resources. We must also rely on science and technology to increase labor productive and commercialize technology. By applying economic levers and market regulation, we must give scientific and technological institutions the capability of self-development and the vitality to serve economic development. We must strengthen the intermediate links in turning scientific research results into productive forces and gradually set up a system of science and technology that supports the sound growth of the entire economy.

7. Select a strategy of educational development that is geared to the needs of modernization, the world, and the future

Students who are now attending colleges, high schools, and primary schools will become a vital new force in the twenty-first century. In the final analysis, the economic competition in the world is a competition of national qualities. The U.S. educational circles have put forward the slogan of training Americans to meet the twenty-first century, underlining the need to strengthen high school and primary school education. The report to the 13th Party Congress also stressed the need to pay attention to educational work and raise the quality of the laborers. In the face of the formidable challenge of the future, we must lay a solid foundation for high school and primary school basic education. We must reform the traditional ideas about education, update the content of education, reform the educational methods, and rearrange the specialties according to the needs of economic and social development. We must widen the students' horizon, increase their ability to blaze new trails and train creative, knowledgeable, and specialized personnel bent on carrying out reform. At the same time, we must attach great importance to the establishment of a lifelong educational system for all people.

8. Giving play to regional comparative advantages to promote common prosperity

With its vast territory and unevenly distributed natural resources, the development of China's productive forces are highly unbalanced. Its economic development forms a gradient structure. We should make rational use of this structure to give play to the comparative economic advantages of various regions. We should have different development objectives and corresponding policies for the coastal and other economically developed areas, for the economically underdeveloped inland areas have no advantages whatsoever in mineral resources, and for economically underdeveloped raw material producing areas and outlying regions. In the regional distribution of industrial development, we should bring into full play the important role of the economically developed regions on the east coast and gradually step up the development of the central and western regions so that all regions can give scope to their comparative advantages and through opening to one another through the exchange of equal values, establish rational regional division of labor and a regional economic structure. In the immediate future, all regions should make earnest efforts to give full play to their comparative advantages, such as high technological level or low labor cost, and they should organize inter-regional lateral economic associations and specialized cooperation so that all kinds of natural, technological, and economic factors can realize optimum regional integration and attain the maximum social benefits. We must pay great attention to the setting up of a modernized industrial structure and the elevation of the scientific and technological level in the underdeveloped regions so that they will become developed regions and achieve common prosperity. The gap in the development of various regions must be reduced step by step.

9. Fix a new investment control strategy

Changing the orientation of investment and adjusting the investment pattern are important means to rationalize the industrial structure, technological structure, and personnel structure. China's present investment system is mainly based on free allocations from the state budget and efforts should be made to change allocations into loans, that is, to make bank loans the main form of investment and gradually increase the role of banks in capital construction investment. Under the present situation in which the price system has not yet been rationalized, we should make use of financial discount interest to create de facto differential interest rates to give guidance to the orientation of investment. In the course of building key projects, we should adopt the competitive bidding system and the contract system. We should expand the decision-making power of enterprises in making investments so that they can invest under the supervision of banks and the guidance of the government departments concerned. We should carry out unified control of investments for equipment updating and technological revamp and investment for capital construction in order to increase the economic effect of investments. We should set up authoritative consultancy organizations for project investment to assist in the macro-economic control and micro-economic guidance of investments. Efforts should be made to make the application, evaluation, examination, and approval of loan projects more scientific, democratic, and institutionalized. It is necessary to learn from the experience of foreign holding companies and in conjunction with China's national conditions, set up all kinds of holding companies of our own.

10. A modern economy open both domestically and externally

Internal opening coordinates with external opening. Internal opening is designed to promote the creation of a unified socialist market and to set up a market system. The socialist market system includes not only commodity markets for consumer goods and means of production but should also include markets for essential factors of production, such as funds, labor service, technology, information, and real estate. Commodity markets alone cannot bring into full play the role of the market mechanism. The socialist market system must allow competition and be open in order to facilitate the development of domestic rational division of labor and to promote international trade. In trade with other countries, it is necessary to realize the optimum foreign trade structure and foreign trade system, to evaluate products with international market prices, to give priority to those industries which make large foreign exchange earnings, and to make efforts to improve the quality of export products. To raise the quality of exports, we must unify the quality standards for products sold on the domestic market with those of export products. China has huge domestic markets. The quality of export products can be assured only when the quality demand of products sold in the domestic markets is the same as that of products sold abroad. We must change the export pattern, increasing our competitive capacity and our ability to earn foreign exchange through exports. Under the unified management, we should allow enterprises engaged in export trade to have a better grasp of the trends in the international market and foreign methods of operation. The administrative organs of various ministries and commissions should follow overall international technological and economic developments, study how to bring domestic comparative advantages into full play, and do better organizational work in product development and the export of resources and equipment. They should improve the control by such economic levers as customs duties, subsidies, exchange rates, and licenses and do a better job in importing foreign funds. While importing foreign funds, attention should be paid in particular to the import of technology and advanced management knowhow and to the assimilation and creative use of imported technology. Efforts should be made to expand the scale of economic and technological exchange and cooperation with other countries to achieve multilateral trade. The foreign trade strategy should change from regulating the surpluses and shortages to making substitutes for imports and then to taking exports as the orientation.

11. Reform of the economic structure

All the above-mentioned projections have to be realized through the reform of the economic structure. The Decision of the Central Committee of the Communist Party of China on Reform of the Economic Structure, adopted by the 12th Party Central at its Third Plenary Session explicitly stated that the socialist economy is a planned commodity economy based on public ownership. This is a scientific thesis made by our Party regarding the socialist economy, a major development of Marxism and the principal basis for our country's economic structural reform. The main task for continued deepening of the reform is to carry out supporting reforms in planning, investment, materials, finance, banking, and foreign trade by centering on the key link of changing the operation mechanism of enterprises and gradually building up the basic framework of a new system based on a planned commodity economy. The essence of the economic structural reform is to adjust the relations of production so that they can suit and promote the growth of the productive forces. In line with the principle of separating ownership from managerial authority, we should invigorate the enterprises owned by the whole people, or state-owned enterprises, promote the development of various sectors of the economy and diversify methods of operation, create an environment of competition on equal footing for enterprises in all forms of ownership, and gradually enable workers and staff to hold shares in state enterprises in order to strengthen their economic ties with the enterprises and increase their sense of responsibility as masters of the enterprise. In this way, we can raise funds and build enterprises in a community in which the state, the collective, and individuals share the risks and the benefits. This will arouse the enthusiasm and initiative of the workers and staff to improve the operation of the enterprises.

In regard to state enterprises, it is necessary to invigorate them and give them certain guidance. Otherwise, there will appear the deviation of overstressing workers' welfare to the neglect of the interests of the state. Some enterprises can consider establishing boards of directors composed of representatives of state interests, enterprise interests, and the interests of the shareholders to be in charge of making strategic decisions for the enterprises and the appointment and removal of directors and managers.

With regard to distribution, we should change the egalitarianist tendencies and prevent the ills of unfair distribution and adopt measures that will truly embody the principle of distribution according to work and achieving common prosperity.

12. The policy system

To achieve our objectives of economic and social development, it is necessary to have a set of scientific and coordinated policies that are conducive to the development of the socialist commodity economy. Policy is a means by which the state gives macro-economic guidance, control, and regulation of economic, scientific, technological, and social development as well as a lever to handle properly the relations between the state, the collective, and individuals. It should be both effective and flexible and should embrace all economic activities of the country. Under the conditions of a socialist planned commodity economy, it is all the more necessary to have a set of effective policies that can regulate economic activities.

The entire society and the entire national economy is a very complicated, colossal system. All factors in the economic field are interlinked and interdependent. In the course of adjusting their operation mechanism, we need both strategic policies and tactical policies, both policies to solve macro-economic problems and policies to solve micro-economic problems. In economic activities, the control over production, circulation, consumption, and domestic and foreign trade all needs corresponding policies. These policies should form an organic whole, a complete policy system. The guidelines for designing the policy system should be the overall strategy of our country's economic and social development.

China's overall development strategy should effectively promote the growth of the productive forces, stimulate the switch to intensive operation, ensure sustained and stable economic growth, continue reform and opening to the outside world, and provide for coordinated economic, scientific, technological and social development.

CHAPTER X
CHINA'S SELECTION
OF STRATEGIES

Section 1
Concerning the Policy System

1. Policies are needed to obtain objectives

The economic, scientific, technological, and social systems of a country are complicated, gigantic systems which require corresponding policies to attain their respective objectives. Policies do not exist in isolation. They form a system of policies which are mutually complementary and condition one another.

Our policy system is formulated in light of the objectives of the development strategy, the targets of the economic structural reform, and the requirements of our country's long-term development. As development is achieved in stages, policies have to be modified constantly while maintaining their continuity. The guidance plan mainly depends on policy to give guidance to the market. Thus it can be said that policy is a link which ties the plan and the market, it is the key to the invigorating and effective management of the economy. The policy system should be like an interwoven network covering all social and economic activities. While drawing up various policies, it is necessary to maintain the unity, continuity, and stability of the central government policies and to have certain amount of flexibility in their execution by various regions, departments, enterprises, and institutions in light of their own specific conditions. In their implementation, policies must include adequate consideration of the timing and conditions,

220

and scientific arrangements in accord with the objective conditions which must be created in order to enforce their implementation.

To attain the objectives of the development strategy and the targets of the economic structural reform, we should choose the right set of policies from among different schemes. Whether or not the correct policy measures are selected determines the extent to which the reform can be carried out, the policies can be coordinated, and the objectives of the economic development can be realized.

2. The economic, scientific, technological, and social development policies, and economic management policies

Industrial policy is the core of the development policy. Besides these, there are policies on industrial distribution and urbanization, foreign economic relations and trade, population and employment, education, and science and technology.

The economic management policy system includes policies on price, finance, banking, foreign trade, foreign exchange, and on the stimulation of enterprises vitality and the controllability of enterprise behavior as well as relevant policies propelling the change of functions of economic management departments.

There should coordination between various policies for development and various policies for reform, and the two kinds of polices should also support each other to form a policy system.

3. The selection of policies

The relation between the steps of reform and policies in coordination with them is an interdependent one. As required by a planned commodity economy, a set of policies which conform to the law of value and support each other can surely give play to the role of various economic levers, make full use of all economic resources, and assure the smooth growth of the socialist economy.

The vigorous development of the socialist planned commodity economy demands that banks play a major role in regulating the circulation of funds and exercising macro-economic control. However, the present pattern of income distribution requires that the banks maintain the allocation of loans as the main form of funds distribution. The new development strategy calls for changes in the pattern of economic development; strengthening of the infrastructure; vigorous promotion of tertiary industries; the development of mutually supplementary trade by bringing the comparative advantages of various regions into full play; rationalization of the consumption pattern, modernization of the industrial structure, and promotion of diversification in people's lives; and increase of enterprise vitality, promotion of enterprise reorganization and association and radical improvement of economic returns. The varied pattern of development cannot be achieved by sticking to the existing form of investment distribution. It is necessary for enterprises to give full scope to their initiative in investment and operation to ensure supply that meets the demand in people's lives and the development of production. This requires reform of the methods of management.

In handling the relations between various policies, it is necessary to adopt the method of system engineering to make advance analysis of the conditions, results, and risks in the implementation of various policies and measures and to appraise the policy supporting schemes. For instance, in 1985 we studied the policy system of China's Seventh Five-Year Plan and made comparisons between two policy schemes. To facilitate understanding of some of the considerations in the study of the policy system, we give the following brief sketch of the two schemes.

The first scheme is one for coordinated reform. Its guiding principle is to focus on the pattern of income distribution, steadily switch over to indirect control, and see to it that no difficult problems are left for continued reform in the future. The degree of maturity in the application of the economic levers determines the course for the adoption of flexible measures, and appropriate flexible measures will constantly create new economic levers and new behavior mechanisms. Administrative measures are applied to show enterprises the correct orientation and guide them to pay attention to medium- and long-term interests. As the application of the economic levers becomes increasingly mature, administrative intervention is steadily reduced. The decision-making structure and motivation structure of enterprises will be solved gradually. As an alternative, we can adopt the method of separating ownership from managerial authority so that the managers have more say in making decisions. The second scheme is a single-item promoting one. It is characterized by a fast pace in the lifting of price control, a situation under which other reforms cannot be carried out in coordination and excessive administrative intervention has to be retained; enterprises are induced to consider short-term benefits; and it is hard to control consumption funds. Although the total output value of industry and agriculture grows at a rapid rate in the immediate future, an equilibrium of major proportions can hardly be achieved. This will likely lead to either of two results: immature reform measures and economic levers trotted out in a hurry which upset the steps of the reform and bring about reversals and instability; or reform that has to be suspended to carry out a major readjustment, causing losses to the national economy.

We recommended the first scheme and put forward our design for the policy system in accordance with this scheme. This demonstrates the importance of policy selection and coordination. It also shows that it is necessary to plan the basic framework of the policy system in advance. The study and formulation of the policy system is a dynamic course with feedback mechanism which requires a large amount of work, particularly quantitative analysis. Such work is the focus of the guidance plan.

The formulation and enforcement of a practical policy system will make it possible for us to make significant advances towards changing the economic pattern and reform of the economic structure. Our policy system should promote development and should be filled with the vitality of reform. At the same time, it should be reliable and highly adaptable. A sound policy system can bring about the macro-economic environment we expect. The vitality of the enterprises will increase considerably. The state's abilities in the areas of macro-economic control, regulation, and management will be strengthened substantially. Of course, the state has to retain a certain amount of administrative intervention to be used in coordination with the policy system. This is essential to reducing the risks of reform.

The macro-economic policy system has to be constantly improved in practice. The lower level policy system guided by it should also be formulated to form a complete and sound scientific policy system. This, coupled with the legal system and the means of auditing, will bring a new look to China's economic management.

Section 2
China's Selection of Strategies

In the foregoing section we have dealt with the concept of the policy system, not the system itself. In our advance towards the future, we are confronted with the selection of various strategies. After a strategy is fixed, corresponding policies are required to carry it out. Both development and reform face the problem of selecting strategies. The following is an attempt to expound the importance of strategy selection through the choosing of major strategy for development.

1. The selection of the "quadrupling" strategy

The strategic objective of China's economic development by the end of this century fixed at the 12th Party Congress is, while steadily working for more and better economic results, to quadruple the 1980 gross annual output value of industrial and agricultural production.

There are many ways to realize the grand objective of quadrupling the 1980 industrial and agricultural output value, but the results are different. In other words, the adoption of one strategic scheme will result in rapid increase of the national strength and greater material benefits for the people, while the adoption of another strategic scheme will result in a slow increase in national strength and little material benefits for the people.

We studied a variety of schemes for economic development and made comparisons between them. The first one is a scheme for balanced development. While working for more and better economic results and while striving for a relatively high growth rate of the gross industrial and agricultural output value, the GNP, and the national income, the people will obtain more material benefits, the economic structure becomes basically rational, and the ratios between infrastructure industries, such as transport and communications, and processing industries, and between agriculture, light industry and heavy industry become appropriate. Attention is given to the development of service trades. The economy maintains steady and sustained growth. The average annual growth rate of the GNP, the national income, and the gross industrial and agricultural output value are projected to be 7.7 percent, 7.1 percent, and 7.3 percent respectively, and the accumulation rate is set at 29 percent.

The second scheme is one of "heavy" structure. It adheres to the principle of attaching importance to heavy industry. Poor economic results affect the growth rate of both production and the standard of living. The average annual growth rate of the GNP, the national income, and the gross industrial and agricultural output value is projected to be 7.2 percent, 6.5 percent, and 7.2 percent respectively, and the accumulation is supposed to be 32 percent.

The third one is characterized by a high-speed economic growth. Its prerequisites are the same as the first scheme, but it demands a high growth rate and an accumulation rate of 35 percent. Although the forecast results for both production and people's lives will reach a fairly high level by 2000, this will be achieved at the expense of the people's immediate interests. The average annual growth rate of the GNP, the national income and the gross industrial and agricultural output value is projected to be 8.9 percent, 8.3 percent, and 8.5 percent.

The implementation of all three schemes can attain or even overfulfill the "quadrupling" objective, but as the roads to development are different, the prospects of development will differ enormously.

With the implementation of the first scheme, China's GNP by 2000 will reach 1,977 billion yuan, 4.4 times that of 1980; the gross industrial and agricultural output value will reach 2,950 billion yuan, 4.1 times that of 1980; national income will reach 1,450 billion yuan, 3.9 times that of 1980; and the average per-capita consumption of the residents will reach 712 yuan, 3.1 times that of 1980. The data show that while attaining the "quadrupling" objective, the implementation of the first scheme will enable the country's economic strength to grow substantially, the people's living standard to rise considerably, and the people's material benefits to expand greatly. In the next decade, the national economy will be able to achieve a stable, sustained, high-speed growth, and there will be harmonious relationships between the development of the national economy and the people's living standard.

With the implementation of this scheme, the agricultural output value will increase by 3.2 times, but its proportion in the entire industrial structure will drop. Meanwhile, the internal structure of agriculture will be adjusted with the proportion of crop farming declining while that of animal husbandry and aquatic breeding going up. The weak links in the national economy, such as energy, transport, building materials, and post and telecommunications, will develop considerably, easing the strain on the infrastructure by a certain degree. The output of electricity will increase 5.7 times; transport, and post and telecommunications, 5.5 times; and the newly rising industries and the electronics industry will grow still faster. Commerce and service trades will expand by wide margins, increasing 6.2 times. In this way, China's industrial structure will approach the standard required of modernization and keep pace with the growth trend of the industrial structure of the industrialized countries.

The implementation of the second scheme will bring about a situation in which the economic structure remains irrational and both the growth of the national economy and the rise of the people's standard of living will be slow. Calculations show that according to the second scheme, China's GNP will reach 1,810 billion yuan by 2000, four times that of 1980; the gross industrial and agricultural output value will reach 2,887 billion yuan, four times that of 1980; the national income will be 1,290.6 billion yuan, 3.5 times that of 1980. Obviously, all indexes in this scheme are lower than those of the first scheme. It is a scheme with more input, less output, and poor macro-economic results.

With the implementation of the third scheme, the GNP will reach 2,475 billion yuan by 2000, 5.5 times that of 1980; the gross industrial and agricultural output value will reach 3,690 billion yuan, 5.4 times that of 1980; national income will be 1,800 billion yuan, 4.9 times that of 1980; the average per-capita consumption of residents will be 790 yuan, 3.5 times that of 1980. Judging from these figures, the third scheme will bring about a greater development of the national economy and greater increases in various indexes while ensuring the realization of the goal of quadrupling the gross industrial and agricultural output value. However, calculations show that in the course of carrying out this scheme, the people's standard of living will register only a meager rise before 1994, and it is only after 1995 that the living standard would improve more quickly. Compared with the first scheme, the enforcement of the third scheme would come at the expense of the people's immediate interests. This will inevitably dampen the people's enthusiasm to a certain extent and the expected results of its implementation will be hard to realize. If the people's living standard is to rise in the immediate future, considerable inflation will emerge which will affect the course of development and the reform.

According to the above analysis, the first scheme is a positive and reliable one that will bring prosperity to the country and the people because it ensures not only the realization of the objective of quadrupling the gross industrial and agricultural output value by the year 2000, but also guarantee a sustained, corresponding rise in the people's standard of living. Therefore, we proposed adoption of the first scheme as basis for the formulation of the strategy and policies for our national economic development.

2. Changes in the consumption level and the strategy to deal with it

(a) The consumption level and the distribution of consumption power

According to calculations on the basis of forecasts made in

line with 1980 prices, the average per-capita consumption level of urban and rural residents throughout the country will be about 712 yuan by the end of this century, more than three times the 227 yuan of 1980, with an average annual increase of 5.9 percent. Of this, the average consumption level of urban residents will be higher than 1,200 yuan and that of rural residents will exceed 600 yuan. This consumption level is apparently lower than that of the developed countries in the same period. However, as China's consumption pattern and price system are different from those of the West, the actual gap between our consumption level and that of the developed countries is far smaller than that indicated by these figures.

Taking the country as a whole, the consumption level is distributed in the form of a gradient, with regional differences bigger than those between town and country. By the end of this century, the level of the rural areas in the outlying districts of western China will still lag behind that of the developed coastal provinces by 10-15 years, while the ratio of consumption level between country and town will be about 1:1.8.

The consumption level of people in city suburbs is higher than that of the city proper, while that of the city proper is higher than that of the surrounding countryside. With regard to the management system, forms of employment, the manner of consumption, the farmers in suburbs enjoy the advantages of the city and the country, and their standard of living is not only higher than the rural areas in general but is also higher than that of the city districts. The residents of the city proper have a wider scope of expenses, and thus their standard of living will be lower than that of the suburban areas.

(b) The characteristics of the changes in consumption power

In the rural areas, reliance on increasing the output of agricultural products will be shifted to reliance on the transfer of the agricultural population to non-agricultural occupations and intensive farming; while in the cities, the reliance on increasing the ratio of employed people will be shifted to reliance on wage increases. Between 1957 and 1981, more than 90 percent of the rise in the consumption level was attributable to increased employment. At present, each of the urban workers and staff shoulder a family burden of 1.7 persons on the average, and there is little room for further reduction. In the future, a higher consumption level must be achieved by means of raising the wages through increased labor productivity.

With the gradual rise of the consumption level, "lump sum" purchases have rapidly increased. Before the Third Plenary Session of the 11th Party Central Committee, the Chinese people with their low income and low consumption pattern, spent most of their income on buying consumer goods for daily use. The money they could accumulate for "lump sum" purchases was confined to 100 yuan or so. Since then a radical change has taken place. Market sales show that people's purchases have shifted from wrist watches, bicycles, and sewing machines (costing about 100 yuan or so apiece) to color TV sets and refrigerators (at the 1,000 yuan level) and are moving to whole sets of family furniture costing several thousand yuan. In the five years between 1978 and 1983, the people's savings deposits more than quadrupled. To meet the growing trend of consumption, it is necessary to open new areas of consumption. Commercialization of housing is an important area in this respect.

(c) In the course of the transformation from low income and low consumption to medium-level income and medium-level consumption and in the process of the economic structural reform, we should adopt the tactics of absorption, transformation, and control with the stress laid on the first two points to cope with the rapid increase in the consumption power. To be specific, we should open up new areas of consumption, expand the traditional areas of consumption, and encourage effective consumption to absorb the excess consumption power and create a reservoir of consumption power; we should transform a part of individual income into accumulation funds through fund raising channels; and we should improve and tighten the means of macro-economic control centering on taxation to regulate the growth rate of consumption funds and accumulate financial resources necessary for the state.

Increasing labor productivity is the basis for raising the wage level and the key to reducing inflation.

As the gaps in regional differences are likely to widen and the differences in the income of various groups of people will increase, we should adopt effective measures to ensure the gradual rise of the living standard of people in low-income regions and of low-income groups in order to achieve common prosperity.

3. The selection of an energy conserving industrial structure and increasing energy utilization efficiency through technological upgrading

China's energy supply faces grim prospects. According to forecasts, if the country's gross industrial and agricultural output value in 2000 quadruples that of 1980, the demand for primary energy will be 1.56 billion tons of standard coal at the low projection and 1.8 billion tons of standard coal at the higher projection. But by then the country's actual energy output will between 1.23 billion and 1.4 billion tons of standard coal. This will leave a shortage of 330 to 400 million tons of standard coal.

Forecast with another method predicts that if the output of energy can only increase by 100 percent instead of the expected 150 percent, the GNP in the year 2000 will be 28.5 percent less than the planned figure, national income will be 31.1 percent less, and the gross industrial and agricultural output value will be 28 percent less. This points to the fact that trying all ways and means to increase energy supplies and striving for marked improvement in the grave situation of energy shortage is an important problem in China's economic and social development.

What is the solution to this energy shortage? We have the following recommendations:

(a) Readjust the industrial structure to turn it from an energy-consuming type into an energy-saving type. We should readjust high energy-consuming industries to reduce their percentage of the entire industrial setup and increase substantially the proportions of the output value of the low energy-consuming food and textile industries as well as the newly rising industries and the tertiary industries to form an energy-saving economic structure. Calculations show that in this structure, a low energy growth rate can support a high national economic growth rate. Concentrated efforts should be made to develop information, electronics, new materials, and other newly rising industries which can promote technological progress and consume less energy and raw materials and have high output value. The coastal cities should make use of their superiorities in technology and labor force to develop processing with imported materials. This is also a way to achieve low energy consumption and high output value.

Proceeding from our national conditions of having a large population calling for employment and a shortage of energy, China should make energetic efforts to develop labor-intensive industries which consume less energy and generate great output value.

To choose an appropriate "light" industrial structure inevitably leads to the establishment of a corresponding import and export structure, namely, in terms of export products the proportion of light industrial and food products increases. This requires an increase in the competitive power of these exports, which will allow them to compete successfully in world markets.

Of course, a "light" industrial structure is incompatible with the demand for the industrialization of a big country. Therefore, this structure can only be developed to an appropriate level as a way to solve the problem of energy shortages.

(b) Obtain more energy supply through technological upgrading and conduct energy conservation in depth and scope. This is the direction for the internal development of our economy as well as the main orientation for directing our energy conservation efforts. Most of the machinery and equipment in our country are outdated and have low efficiency and high energy consumption. China's energy consumption for every 10,000 U.S. dollars of output value was as high as 2.5 tons of standard coal, the highest in the world. Therefore, we should be determined to make painstaking efforts to conduct technological upgrading, particularly the renovation and updating of the major energy consuming equipment such as boilers, pumps, power generation equipment, and internal combustion engines.

Secondly, we should spare no effort in supporting the scientific research in new energy-saving technologies and widely apply the effective technologies to solve the problem of energy shortages. In our scientific and technological work, we should give priority to the study and popularization of energy-saving technologies.

Economizing on the use of raw materials, raising product quality, and increasing labor productivity are indirect ways to conserve energy. We recommend integration of direct with indirect energy conservation, and of energy conservation with increasing economic returns so as to obtain the maximum economic returns with the minimum amount of energy. China has enormous potentials for energy conservation in the broad sense of the term. According to estimates, our potential for energy conservation is about 52 percent, of which the potential for direct energy conservation accounts for one-third and that of indirect energy conservation two-thirds. By fully tapping these potentials, it is possible for us to achieve the objective of quadrupling our industrial and agricultural output value by the end of this century with an increase of 100 percent in our energy output.

4. Reinforce the weakest links in our national economy—transport and communications

Transport and communications are the weakest links in our national economy at present as well as the bottleneck in our future national economic development. To change this state of affairs, it is necessary to adopt the following measures:

(a) Reform the transport system—We must put an end to the situation in which transport service is monopolized by the state and adopt the policy of pooling the resources of the state, the localities, the collectives, individuals, and foreign funds to engage in developing the transport industry, thus bringing about a coordinated development of railway, highway, water transport, air transport, and pipeline transport and increasing the capacity of comprehensive transport network. We must encourage competition between a variety of means of transport and manners of operation.

The transport construction projects can be undertaken and managed by the central government, the local authorities, the collectives, or individuals in accordance with their place, role, and service scope in the national economy. Some projects can be built and managed by Chinese-foreign joint ventures or solely foreign-funded enterprises.

(b) Readjust charges for transport services and reform the materials supply and distribution system—Readjusting the charges for transport services will help change the transport structure and will promote enterprises to increase their economic results. For example, increasing the fares for short-distance railway transport can reduce the burden on railway transport facilities. In areas where railway and water transport parallel each other, the introduction of flexible transport fares will encourage the transport of large quantities of materials by water.

Reform the materials and equipment supply and distribution system will help avoid counterflow, detours, repetition, and fruitless transport. It is necessary to carry out rational coordination of the production, transport, and marketing of coal, cement, chemical fertilizer, iron and steel, and grain on the basis of comprehensive techno-economic analysis in order to ease the strain transport industry.

(c) Strengthen comprehensive control and increase investment returns—At present, China has inadequate investment in transport, and its use is in many cases irrational. One of the main causes for this state of affairs is the separate management of transport by various departments. It is thus necessary to gradually reduce and merge the organizations in charge of transport and set up comprehensive organs in charge of transport services. Their main functions would be to study transport development strategy, make overall arrangements for the planning and building of transport facilities, study and formulate major policies for transport industry, make use of economic means to organize and coordinate the comprehensive development of various modes of transport and play a supervising role, and plan the use of investments and carry out appraisals and examination of such projects.

The following measures should be adopted to improve communications:

(a) Bringing into full play the initiative of various quarters—Under unified planning we should adopt various manners of operation in developing communications. International communication should be run exclusively by the central government under the management of a single department. Long-distance communication should mainly be run by the central government, with other forms of management permitted in a limited way. Urban communication should be mainly run by the state and managed by the department in charge or run jointly with the local authorities. In the rural areas, all forms of operation should be permitted and developed.

(b) Adopting the policy of supporting communication enterprises—We should reform and exercise unified control over the prices of communication services. The products, services, and special tasks undertaken by communication enterprises have to be paid for, and the prices must be calculated according to quantity and quality. High depreciation rates should adopted for state communication enterprises so as to speed up their technological innovation and upgrading. The state should give priority to construction projects in communications, and funds for these projects can be raised by means of joint operation, the issue of bonds, and other methods.

(c) Giving energetic support in advanced technology—To speed up the modernization of communications undertakings, we should adopt the policy to relax control on the import of communication technology and communication equipment, and spare no effort to foster development of domestic communication technology and the communication equipment manufacturing industry.

(d) In regard to certain special requirements of communications undertakings, we should study and work out explicit laws, regulations, and methods to create conditions for the rational organization of communications network, comprehensive use of all means of communication, and wide application of advanced communication technology.

5. Three strategies for scientific and technological development

In face of the challenge posed by the new worldwide technological revolution, there are three possible strategic ways in handling the relations between China's traditional technology and high technology.

The first strategy is to develop traditional technology and, after having accumulated certain economic strength, proceed to develop high technology, in other words, to concentrate funds and other resources on developing traditional technology first.

This strategy is in keeping with our techno-economic and management level at the present stage and is likely to attain a high growth rate. By 2000, our objective of quadrupling the gross output value of industry and agriculture can be attained. By that time, however, the technological gap between our country and the developed countries will further widen, and China will inevitably go through a large-scale readjustment of its industrial structure for which we may have to pay a heavy price. As a result, our growth rate in the early twenty-first century will be slowed down, landing us in an awkward situation. Therefore, this development strategy is inadvisable.

The second strategy is to direct our main efforts to the development of high technology and at the same time pay attention to the development of traditional technology. This is a development strategy which the developed countries began to adopt in the 1970s.

According to this strategy, by 2000 our gap with developed countries will be narrowed in certain key high-tech fields, such as microelectronics technology and optical fiber communication. However, owning to our limitations in funds and scientific and technological knowledge, our gap with the developed countries will further widen in most areas. Our infrastructure facilities and culture and education will not be fully developed and thus cannot meet the needs of development of high technology. Meanwhile, the basic needs of the country's economic development and the people's lives continue to rely on the development of traditional industries and technologies. Under these circumstances, it will be difficult to achieve the objective of quadrupling the gross industrial and agricultural output value by 2000. Due to the low technological level of our traditional industries, our export products lack competitive power in the international market. Therefore, this strategy is also inadvisable.

The third strategy is to devote our main efforts to the development of traditional technology and give equal attention to traditional technology and high technology in scientific research and the import of technology; to develop high technologies, with electronic information technology in the lead; to transform traditional industries and traditional technologies; to change the existing state of traditional technology and create a large number of mixed technologies which integrate high technology with traditional technology. This is also called the strategy of "mixed technologies." It requires that the development of traditional technologies embodies the factors of high technology.

The "mixed technology" strategy includes the following two stages of development. During the first stage (the period of the Seventh Five-Year Plan and the early stage of the Eighth Five-Year Plan), vigorous efforts will be made to develop traditional industries, and high technologies (mainly electronics and information technologies) will be used to transform traditional industries.

During the second stage (from the middle of the Eighth Five-Year Plan to the period of the Ninth Five-Year Plan), the main efforts will be directed to adapting to the "mixed technology" system and to completing industrialization on the basis of the integration of high technology with traditional technology. In this way, we can switch the focus of development to high technology in the twenty-first century. We recommend adopting this kind of scientific and technological development strategy.

These are a small part of the strategic problems and policies mentioned in "China Towards the Year 2000." We have cited them as examples of the study of the strategies and policies which China should adopt. It is impossible for us to expound on all the problems included in this gigantic research project. Our study is only an attempt to help in the formulation of China's policy system, which is of vital importance to our country as it is in the middle of an economic structural reform.

CONCLUDING REMARKS

We are exploring and creating a model of socialist modernization with Chinese characteristics. It is a gigantic engineering project reflecting the features of our time. This magnificent undertaking in human history can hardly be summed up in one book. In our view, by linking up the national conditions, scenarios, strategies, and policies and giving them dialectical deliberations, we can draw the contours of the China of tomorrow and its splendid prospects for modernization.

Our study indicates that so long as we advance unswervingly along the correct road shown by the Party Central Committee, the task of quadrupling the GNP and enabling the people to enjoy a fairly comfortable standard of living by the end of this century can surely be fulfilled. By then, China will have become a powerful socialist country with political stability, economic prosperity, and substantial national strength. Its people will live in peace and happiness. We shall display to the whole world a model of socialism with Chinese characteristics and full of vigor and vitality. Filled with confidence, China is forging ahead to a bright future.

We are firmly convinced that by the middle of the next century, we can catch up with and even outstrip the moderately developed countries and basically achieve modernization. By the end of the twenty-first century, it is possible for us to catch up with the developed countries and realize the long-cherished aspirations of the Chinese nation. The twenty-first century will mark the dawn of a new age for our country.

中国走向2000年

王慧炯 李伯溪 著

*

新世界出版社出版

外文印刷厂印刷

中国国际图书贸易总公司发行

中国北京车公庄西路21号

北京邮政信箱第399号 邮政编码100044

1989年（英）第一版

ISBN 7-80005-092-0／Z·022

01000

17-E-2489P